The Beauty of Tribulation

J. A. Cox

J.A. Cox
Wilmington, Delaware

J.A. Cox/ J.A. Cox
1207 Delaware Ave #2615
Wilmington, DE, 19806
jacoxbtih@gmail.com
www.jacoxbtih.com

Book Layout ©2013 BookDesignTemplates.com

Cover photo by Gerd Altmann from Pixabay
Cover design by J.A. Cox

Ordering Information:
Quantity sales. Special discounts are available on quantity purchases by corporations, associations, and others. For details, contact the "Special Sales Department" at the address above.

The Beauty of Tribulation/ J. A. Cox. —1st ed.
ISBN 978-0-9895773-2-8

Contents

This book is dedicated to all those who supported me during my darkest hour and the Lord for his love, goodness and mercy.

The Love of God is like a tsunami that hits you like a feather.

—J. A.

CHAPTER 1

At A Glance

Tribulation is the most abundant commodity that everyone is looking to sell but no one is willing to buy. It is an experience so common to mankind that it transcends social, cultural and language barriers. It requires no introduction or explanation.

We commonly associate the following with it:

1. Suffering.
2. Adversity.
3. Trial.
4. Pain.
5. Temptation.
6. Infirmity.

It is safe to assume that the general perception of tribulation is not positive, and we desire to avoid it as much as possible. This places a Christian in a precarious position.

This is the case when we consider what God's word exhorts:

1. To count it all joy, James 1:2,3.
2. To greatly rejoice in it, 1 Peter 1:6.
3. To not think of it as strange, 1 Peter 4:12.
4. That we glory in it, Romans 5:3.
5. Paul expressed exceeding joy in it, 2 Corinthians 7:4.
6. We must experience much to enter God's kingdom, Acts 14:22.

In regard to such maybe you have thought the following:

1. Okay Paul, I know you were a great man of God and had endured much hardship but I'm having a difficult time finding joy in this.
2. Is there something wrong with me if I have no joy in suffering?
3. Why must we go through tribulation?
4. Why does God allow us to suffer?
5. Do we experience tribulation as a form of punishment?
6. Does tribulation mean that God has forsaken me?

I realize that these are thoughts believers scatter from as roaches do from the light. This is done out of a fear that entertaining such could give authority to them as well as make it a reality. While there is truth in that line of thought, the realization of that reality is on a conditional basis. In other words, those thoughts would not manifest without effort being put into making them so or a lack of effort to bring them about. There is also an equivalent level of danger in believing that a Christian is above such lines of thinking. It is also devastating to deny their reality. Those types of thoughts are a natural and unavoidable occurrence generated from our unconverted body. Also, another truth needs to be realized, your tribulation is not being orchestrated by God.

A Matter Of Perspective

Understand this, believers and people in general don't always view tribulation in a negative light. This is true when it is painful, humiliating or even exhausting.

Hush my mouth, right. That must have been a Freudian slip.

Relax, it was deliberate. The reason this is so has everything to do with personal gain.

Do you like math?

I know that I am not fond of it, but we will use some basic greater than less than to convey a point.

The following involves tribulation in regard to personal gain:

1. When the view of the tribulation experience is considered *greater than* the view of personal gain this *equals* a rejection of the tribulation being experienced.

2. When the view of the tribulation experience is considered *less than* the view of personal gain this *equals* an acceptance of the tribulation being experienced.

Let's first take a look at some instances that people accept the tribulation being experienced because the view of perceived gain is greater:

1. Our first example is a professional body builder. They are willing to endure agonizing soreness of muscles, perspire heavily, and undergo rigorous training for several hours to obtain their well sculpted body so that they can receive financial compensation, fame and trophies.

2. Next, we have the ambitious entrepreneur. They will exhaust the health of their mind and body and work long hours, even at the cost of depriving loved ones of needed time, to the extent of separation or infidelity. It doesn't matter how obvious the deterioration of their physical health is, they will continue to burn the candle at both ends just to acquire that promotion, million-dollar deal or admiration they are seeking.

3. Let's talk about Thrill seekers. They are willing to go on national television and face their worst fears, suffer public humiliation or even tempt fate attempting death defying feats all in the name of fame or fortune and many times both.

4. Last, we have the expecting mother. Not many women after cuddling with that newborn bundle of joy would not be willing to say the weight gain, dislocated organs, emotional roller coaster and so on was not worth it or that they are not willing to do it all over again for the joy set before them.

Now let's look at some instances in which people reject the tribulation being experienced because the view of perceived gain is less:

1. Let's say that things have been hard financially, and you get a raise, bonus, or just come into a large sum of money and

then all of a sudden, a major repair is needed on the house or vehicle. Why is it that this scenario seems to be tied to financial gain so often right?

2. Perhaps you made plans to meet up with a special someone or go let off some steam with a buddy and as you happily dart out of the house you just so happen to notice that one of your tires are flat or maybe you locked your keys in the vehicle and you don't have a spare.

3. Maybe you are excited to go see family you have not seen in quite some time and the plane tickets are already purchased but you suddenly get urgent news that one of your family members are in ICU and you are asked to get there as soon as possible.

4. Possibly you have been suffering with an infirmity for years and no matter how much you or others have prayed God does not take it away.

In the instances mentioned above, when an individual perceives a much higher personal gain for what they must endure to obtain it tribulation is viewed in a positive light. This is indicative of our human nature for sinner and saint alike, to view tribulation in such a light. Under normal circumstances there is no error in doing so because it is natural. The problem is when we only perceive tribulation in this manner. This is especially so for a Christian in light of what the scriptures that have been shared have to say about tribulation. The question that needs to be addressed is why is it when we don't perceive our gain of reward to be significant enough that we reject the tribulation being experienced?

Let's address some things that distort the believers view of tribulation:

1. We fail to realize that tribulation is not God motivated but a result of the presence of sin in this world.

2. Because of sin: the world is cursed, things must be gained by much labor, disease exists, there is death, there is sorrow, we suffer, we are divided, and natural disasters occur.

3. Even though God initiated the curse, man was warned of the results of his disobedience but rebelled anyway and God by his righteous nature kept true to his word.

4. We have a misinterpretation that just because God blesses our obedience that for some reason we are excluded from further tribulation, God is love after all right.

The greatest problem with Christians in general is just as the ancient Israelites from the fourth plague of flies to the ninth of darkness, we desire to remain in the safety of Goshen while Egypt is destroyed. Here is the news flash, God never intended to leave them in Egypt nor its vicinity, which is why he passed over all the land with that final deadly plague. Also, when we look at Matthew 5:45, we come to understand that the rain falls on both the just and unjust alike. Also, in Matthew 7:25 - 27, we see that both the house of the foolish and wise man was subjected to the rain, floods, and wind. One may respond and say that we are exhorted by God's word that fervent faith based prayer avails much, read James 5: 15,16. We are also provided with the example of Elijah praying for the rain to cease and then later on for it to begin again. God makes it clear that he answers prayers and that is not being spoken against. Scripture clearly tells us to seek, ask and knock as found in Matthew 7:7 and to pray and not faint as it says in Luke 18:1 and that God will avenge those who cry unto him such as stated in Luke 18:7.

However, let's consider this:

1. Just because he answers prayer it doesn't mean the rain will be stopped immediately. The rest of Luke 18:7 says that God will avenge though he bears long with his children.

2. In Matthew 7:7 it does not say after you seek, knock or ask a specified number of times that you will then receive.

3. In the account with Elijah it was not until after the seventh time that his servant checked that he saw the little rain cloud.

4. Paul sought earnestly for the thorn in his flesh to be removed but it was not.

It is clear that God answers prayer. It is also clear that even when he delays or doesn't that we must remember as Isaiah 55:9 says, his ways are higher than ours and 1 Corinthians 2:16 who hath known his mind. In other words, whether we like it or not or understand it or not, things are the way they are because he has a plan that he is working. An essential part of that plan lies in us enduring the tribulation instead of it being resolved. You will come to understand a reason for this as well as gain meaningful answers and conjecture to the negative thoughts and questions surrounding tribulation as we make our way through this book.

CHAPTER 2

Spheres of Influence

We are going to lay a crucial foundation to understand how God uses tribulation in our lives. In order to do this, we will use a theory that I call the Spheres of Influence. The purpose of this theory is to help explain the relationships of nature, animals, spiritual beings and mankind to the influence of God's own divine nature upon them.

Nature

BODY   SPIRIT

UNIQUE NATURE   WILL   DIVINE NATURE

Spirit

This represents the portion of God's essence that is infused into every one of his creations. Within it is a portion of God's divine nature. The divine nature consists of divine awareness, divine dependence, and divine desire. Also, for all of creation the spirit is the seat of reason and intellect, the mind. All knowledge and understanding is of God and this ability in creation is a result of the presence of God's Spirit within.

Does the thought of nature having some kind of reason seem inane?

Well, God responded to Job about the morning stars singing in Job 38:7, Paul explained that creation groans and travails in Romans 8:22, Jesus that the rocks would cry out if man failed to praise him as seen in Luke 19:39, 40 and John was admonished not to write what the thunders uttered during his revelation on the isle of Patmos as it reads in Revelation 10:4.

Body

This represents the vessel God has created to house the spirit. Paul explains in 1 Corinthians 15:38 - 41 that in nature there are terrestrial bodies pertaining to the earth and celestial bodies pertaining to outer space. Within these bodies resides a unique nature. This unique nature consists of self-awareness, self-dependence, and self-desire. This unique nature is the seat of emotion, the heart of nature.

Will

Nature unlike spiritual beings and mankind does not possess a free will. This means that it does not have the authority to reject God and choose to be given over to the affections of its own unique nature. It is at God's command that the snow falls upon the earth as well as the rain as we read in Job 37:6. Also the morning and night are at his command as we see in Job 38:8-12 and we see the winds and sea yield to the rebuke of Christ as we find in Mark 4:39.

Although, when God does directly influence nature such as causing the grounds of the Jordan and Red Sea to be dry for Israel to pass through at other times he doesn't. At the times when he is not nature is governed by its own will. However, the will of nature is in submission to God's divine nature and will fulfill the inherent instruction that God has instilled within its own unique nature. It is an automatic function that it understands and will carry out.

Here are some examples:

Water is governed by a perpetual cycle to nourish the earth with precipitation.

The sun shines continuously at its fixed-point giving light and warmth never making the slightest variation in its distance from the planets revolving around it.

The moon revolves continually around the earth in its fixed interval never making the slightest variation in its perpetual course and bears direct influence on the tides of the sea.

Therefore, God does not need to directly set these into motion on a daily basis because the instruction is inherent within their own unique nature. It is for this reason we can boldly proclaim that they do so at his command.

Does this mean that God is the author of natural disasters?

Absolutely not. Romans 8:20-22 tells us of the agony of creation. Sin is the reason for this pain. The world not only lies in wickedness but is infected with leprous sin that slowly rots it away. This infection is what results in nature's erratic patterns that are contrary to its own design. Although, it is according to the design of the curse of sin that it brings death and destruction along with life. Adam and Eve by the influence of Satan brought about this curse upon all creation, not God.

Animals

BODY   SPIRIT

INSTINCT   WILL   DIVINE NATURE

Spirit

In animals this also houses the divine nature, consisting of divine awareness, divine dependence, and divine desire. This is the seat of reason and intellect, the mind.

Body

This not only houses the spirit but also an instinctive nature. This instinctive nature is the seat of emotion, the heart. It consists of self-awareness, self-dependence, and self-desire. Within the instinctive nature are the unique survival skills for each species to survive in their given environment. Another thing it contains is an understanding of the animals created purpose.

Will

Similar to nature animals don't have the freedom of will to reject God's will. Animals do have the freedom of will to reject or obey the will of mankind. So, the animal's instinctive nature is fully subject unto the divine nature. It is at God's command that the eagles mount up as is found in Job 39:27-30 and at his command the animals entered the Ark as we read in Genesis 7:8,9,15,16. However, like with nature, when God has no specific requirement as going into the Ark or feeding his prophet as seen in 1 Kings 17: 4-6, they are governed by their own instinctive nature. So, when you read scripture about God providing for the lions and ravens like it says in Job 38:39-41, feeding the fowl of the air as stated in Matthew 6:26, this is accomplished by their instinctive nature. As we have learned, God has placed the instructions in their instinctive nature to be carried out using their natural abilities to survive in their given environments. So, we can boldly proclaim that God provides for them.

Spiritual Beings

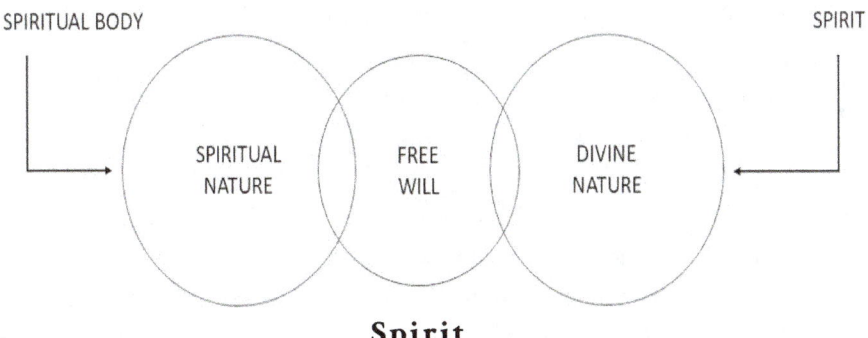

Spirit

This like with nature and animals is the seat of logic and reason, the mind. While the spirit is the mind of all creation, the reasoning ability of nature and animals is not on par with spiritual beings or mankind. Although, as with the others this also houses the divine nature, consisting of divine awareness, divine dependence, and divine desire.

Spiritual Body

Here resides a spiritual nature that consists of self-awareness, self-dependence, and self-desire. This spiritual nature is the seat of emotion or the heart of the spiritual being. A unique attribute of the spiritual body is that it is not subject to the physical laws that govern the rest of creation. Another innate ability it has is that it can manifest in a physical form. We see this in the account with the three men Abraham had conversed with, whom one was God as we read in Genesis 18: 1-3. Also, there is the account of the men in shining garments found at the tomb of Christ seen in Luke 24: 2-5.

Free Will

It functions as a bridge between the spiritual body and the spirit. The influence of the divine nature on the will draws the spiritual body into subjection unto the divine nature but the influence of the spiritual body on the will draws it unto subjection to the spiritual nature. The spirit cannot be corrupted by sin, God's nature is righteous but if the will is subjected to the spiritual body there is only judgment. There is no redemption for spiritual beings. Once the will is lost to the spiritual nature it loses its freedom and is forever in bondage. Biblical proof of this loss of will as it submits to the spiritual nature can be seen in the following scriptures:

1. Satan's rebellion against God in Revelation 12:7-9.
2. Angels chained who left their first estate in Jude 6.
3. Angels who sinned cast into hell in 2 Peter 2:4.
4. Angels chose to have sex with women in Genesis 6:1,2.

While the influence of the divine nature is very great on spiritual beings because of their close proximity and daily interactions with God it is his desire that they choose to yield their will. As we have seen in the illustrations from the scriptures above, proximity alone does not equate to righteousness. The submission of the will along with proximity puts us in a place that will earn God's favor.

Mankind

SOUL

SPIRIT

BODY — HUMAN NATURE — FREE WILL — DIVINE NATURE

Spirit

It is from here that the divine nature exerts its influence. Once again, it consists of divine awareness, divine dependence, and divine desire. This makes the spirit the seat of rationale, the mind. Like with spiritual beings the divine nature gives mankind the ability for logic and reason. It is this mind by which we serve the law of God as found in Romans 7:25. The divine nature is also the conscience of our being, influenced indirectly by God in warnings through dreams, prophecy and feelings of being watched, especially when a person is engaged in secret sin. This influence can be direct or indirect but either way the purpose is to get us to yield to God's will. In an indirectly influenced manner it sounds alarms when our behavior is contrary to the divine nature. This type of influence would be like the depiction of the angel that suddenly appears on the side of the head of a cartoon character enticed by the depiction of a red devil with pitchfork on the other side of their head. Our conscience is limited in regard to our ability to ignore it or become dull to its warning. When that happens and we continue in that wrong behavior pattern it eventually becomes seared as is explained in 1 Timothy 4:1,2. This process happens gradually as the conscience is continually rejected. In the believer the influence of the conscience is boosted by the indwelling of the Holy Ghost, but it is still capable of being seared.

Soul

It is in subjection to the affections of the body and things that effect the body. This is so in the fallen state of man that the soul by default resides in this condition and is considered dead. In this state it is ruled by the human nature that resides there. This human nature consists of self-awareness, self-dependence, and self-desire. Thereby, the soul is the emotional seat of our being, our heart. Since the soul is dead in our fallen state this makes our heart wicked. This wickedness deceives the will from yielding to the influence of the divine nature fulfilling the description in Jeremiah 17:9 about it being deceitful above all things and out of it proceeding evil thoughts as we read in Matthew 15:19. Further biblical proof lies in the fact that once the soul is separated from the body the full range of emotions is still present. In Luke 16: 19-31 after the rich man's soul separated from his body and descended into hell he was in torment, thirsted, cried and prayed. Not only that, he had all of the senses, sight, hearing, taste, touch and speech. In our fallen state both the body and soul are dead in trespasses and sin, but the soul can be redeemed. The body remains in a permanent fallen condition until the rapture if the will remains in subjection unto God until that time or death. This means that the soul can be overtaken and die if the will is subjected to human nature and given back over to the affections of the body.

Free Will

It is the bridge between the soul and spirit. The influence of the divine nature on the will draws the soul into subjection unto God and a relationship of servitude. The influence of human nature on the will causes interference in order to diminish the influence of God's divine nature on the soul. Once more, the spirit is incorruptible by sin because of God's divine nature. The spirit also cannot be tempted, overcome by evil or be destroyed as the soul can for the same reasons. What happens is, the influence is diminished from the divine nature upon the will the more that it is drawn toward the human nature. Just as God draws near as we do like it says in James 4:8 he will also do the opposite, proving that God as our master equals servitude. When the will is subject unto human nature it is in a state of bondage or slavery. In this state a person is given over to the various affections of the body. What needs to be understood is that the will of spiritual beings and mankind are both free to choose submission to God's divine nature or to reject it altogether. Neither nature or animals have such liberty.

Body

It was formed from the earth and houses the soul and spirit as we are told in Genesis 2:7 and made in the image of God as it says in Genesis 1:27. The organ that is under the direct influence of our spirit and soul is the brain.

Brain

Left Hemisphere- influenced by the spirit. The diminished influence of the divine nature is reduced to a simple capacity of logic and reason as far as the body is concerned. The more a person allows their will to be influenced by the divine nature in the fallen state there will be an increase in morality, character and discipline. Basically, good traits that align with logic and reason will be more prevalent. However, the decrease of the influence of the divine nature on this hemisphere leads to

Pharisaical behavior, mockery, scoffing, haughtiness, perfectionism and so on. In our corrupted body the motivating factor for these things is *self-awareness*.

Right Hemisphere - influenced by the soul. The greater the influence of human nature the more emotional an individual will become. Also, there will be a rise in negative emotions such as obsession, rage, revenge, resentment, depression, concupiscence and so on. On the other hand, there will be positive things such as compassion, creativity, empathy, philanthropy, kindness and so on. However, in the fallen state these are motivated by *self-dependence* and *self-desire*.

We see the expression of these influences from these two spheres on the will in the execution of the body's limbs from the head, to the arms, hands, legs, feet and toes. Of course, we know that through action potential in the neurons that electrical signals are activated then hormones are triggered, and those body parts react according to our will. In a most basic way this is the series of events leading to our decision making. However, out of all of our body members there is one through which the influence of our will is most expressed, the tongue. Yes, no other member so easily exposes our most dominant influence than the tongue. It is for this reason it is considered a fire, world of iniquity, an unruly evil and full of deadly poison as we read in James 3:6-8. Neither is any other member so easily yielded to our human nature. This is so in our natural fallen state due to our wicked hearts as read in James 3:14-16.

So, in our fallen state under the limited influence of the divine nature on our left hemisphere of the brain people will only be able to obtain to the stature of Aristotle, Solomon, Einstein and so on. They will acquire just enough of God to amass great logic and intellect but never be able to come to the knowledge of the truth as explained in 2 Timothy 3:7. Now on the right hemisphere the greatest position one may reach is like unto Mother Theresa, Gandhi, Buddha and so on but in either scenario the soul and body will remain dead. Without the indwelling of the Holy Spirit to regenerate the soul people in the above condition will remain under the wrath of God. In the next chapter we will explore how the soul becomes dead with an analogy using the sun and the ocean.

CHAPTER 3

Depths of Separation

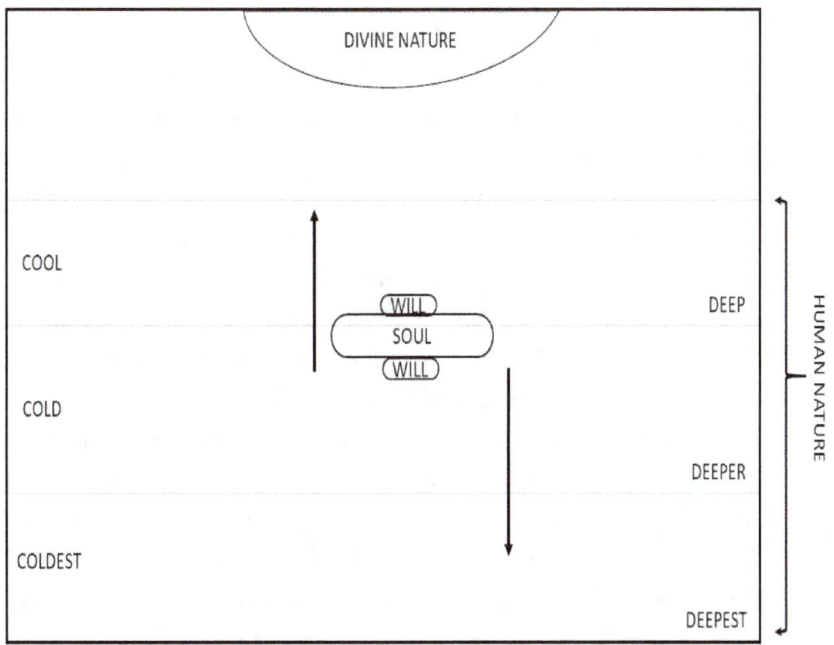

When the sun shines over the oceans its beams of light penetrate down to the deepest depths. In that same manner so does the influence of the divine nature upon the will no matter how deep that human nature may pull the soul. An interesting fact about light is that a single beam consists of three rays. The first of those rays is invisible, the second is visible and the third produces heat. As that light travels through the depths the warmth from the heat is the first to diminish. This happens as the water gets so cold that it no longer has an effect on its surroundings. The second thing to diminish is the visible portion of light as it is neutralized by the darkness of the deeper depths. Last, the first part which is unseen continues to penetrate fathoms deep but since it is unseen and not felt it goes unnoticed. This is the way of the influence of the divine nature on the will of fallen man. The soul and will are one so where goes the will so goes the soul.

Even though the soul is dead in the fallen state the more that it resides in the shallower portion of human nature the greater the influence God's divine nature will have upon it. In this position the soul is closer to being renewed. Just as the light is three parts, so are there three parts of the divine nature: divine awareness, divine dependence and divine desire. Just like light with water, so does the divine nature penetrate to the deepest depths of human nature to reach the will and soul. The deeper the soul has been drawn into human nature the more diminished the influence of God's divine nature will be upon it. The heat which is the first to be neutralized in light is represented by divine desire. The deeper the soul moves toward being reprobate the less concern it will have for what God desires. At that lowest point all shame and remorse is lost as a numbness sets in from the icy surrounding depths, thus the conscience is seared as explained in 1 Timothy 4:2 and they are given over by God not desiring his ways as we read in Romans 1:21-32. The second to go is the visible portion of light represented by divine dependence. This light is engulfed at the lower depths by self-dependence. This is a result of not heading to admonitions such as lean not to your own understanding like we read in Proverbs 3:5-7 and God resists the proud in James 4:6; 1 Peter 5:5 on a repeated basis. When self-dependence eclipses divine dependence there is an automatic rejection from God and that leaves the soul at the mercy of this aspect of human nature. Even though this makes the soul dead in trespasses and sin it can still be reached. A person in this state would be found in-between the deep to deeper depths of separation. Although, just like the invisible portion of light penetrates to the lowest depths so does divine awareness. In the coldest, deepest depths of separation where man has become reprobate the ever-present existence of divine awareness goes unnoticed just like the invisible part of light at the lowest depths of the sea. This happens because it is eclipsed by self-awareness.

On the other-hand, by the drawing of the divine nature upon the will which represents his goodness as we read in Romans 2:4, by hearing his word in Romans 10:17, this brings us back to the brink of salvation. Salvation takes place when we yield our will wholly to his, in other words when we repent as explained in Romans 10:13,9-11. Repentance means a one hundred and eighty degree turn from the path of destruction that we were walking along. Repentance is not just a temporary change in direction but a change in course, a collapsing of the bridges and burning the boats. Meaning, we cut off all pathways leading back the way we came. We do not only receive salvation through repentance which is the cornerstone of the salvation experience but through repentance we become a partaker of the righteousness of Jesus Christ as read in 2 Corinthians 5:21. At this point we receive an indwelling of the Holy Ghost that regenerates the soul but not the body as read in Romans 8:9-17; 2 Corinthians 5:17. Another very unique thing happens at salvation, the soul is baptized into the body of Christ by the Holy Ghost as seen in 1 Corinthians 12:13. It is through this indwelling of the Holy Ghost that the Father and Son abide in us. The result of this is that the divine nature will have a greater influence upon our will. This takes place by the Holy Ghost shielding the soul by strongly inhibiting the affections of the flesh and making it subject unto the divine nature as we are told in Romans 8:10-12. This sanctifies the body, meaning that it is set apart for service unto God even though it is still unconverted as we read in Romans 8:11. Even so the body remains susceptible to the affections of human nature which will try to influence our will and turn us away from God if we yield to it. To better grasp this we will discuss five archetypes.

Christian Archetypes

1. **The Boat** - this represents the life of a newly converted believer. Due to our body being under the influence of its affections it is like a boat jostled by the sea but remaining afloat. A new believer, though they may be pulled by the influences of human nature they are able to resist without being drawn down into its depths. Like a boat jostled by the sea so will they still be buffeted by the whims of the desires of the body but remain afloat.

2. **Peter walking on the sea** - this represents a believer who has yielded their will repeatedly to God's divine nature and exerts more mastery over their human nature. Like Peter with their gaze fixed upon Christ they are unmoved by tumult of the sea.

3. **Jesus asleep on the boat** - this represents a more established Christian resting in the most secret place of the most high as is read in Psalms 91:1. They are so embedded in the Body of Christ that the wicked one toucheth them not as we see in 1 John 5:18. Christ remained at peace although the boat was rocked by the wind and sea and so does a Christian who remains at such a depth in Christ. The winds will blow, the floods will rise, and the rains will fall but like the wise man's house they shall not be removed.

4. **The rebuking Christ** - Although Christ slept, he was awakened by the unbelieving disciples and after his rebuke of nature he rebuked them. Just as Christ's peace was susceptible to disruption so is the very established Christian's. It is due to the incessant influence of human nature upon the will which represents the unbelieving disciples and raging storm for the Christian in this state. However, because they are so entrenched within the Body of Christ as Jesus, they

have the boldness to rebuke the advances of the body upon the will and further yield themselves unto the Lord.

5. **Peter sinking in the sea** - This represents anytime human nature draws the will away from God and plunges it back into the cold depths of separation. It is an inevitable eventuality but like Peter it is not the end of our story unless we allow it to be.

The point I am trying to convey is that while we remain embedded in the body of Christ no man can pluck us from his hand. Just as our will is drawn up from the depths of separation so can it be enticed from within the Body of Christ. This takes place by yielding to seducing spirits and doctrines of devils as explained in 1 Timothy 4:1, who stimulate the natural affections of the body and which we yield to as explained in James 1:14,15. No matter how deep we are in Christ we will still be susceptible to the whims of the unconverted body. It is also just as true that the deeper we are in Christ that the influences and affections of the body will have less of an impact upon us. Although the indwelling of the Spirit plunges us into Christ's body this was never meant by God to be the end of our salvation experience. Before we move on, we need to discuss another essential part of our salvation experience. That essential part is water baptism. It is through water baptism that we become a partaker of the death, burial and resurrection of Jesus Christ as it reads in Romans 6:3-7 and Colossians 2:12. It is also through it that we have the answer of a good conscience toward God as it is explained in 1 Peter 3:21. However, neither does this complete our salvation experience. This will be discussed in more depth in the final chapter.

Where It Fits

In order to get our first glimpse of how tribulation plays a role in all of this we are going to look at our fallen nature from birth. We realize that children are born into this world with an inherent inclination to do bad as it says in Psalms 51: 5. This means children are born with a will that is enslaved to their human nature. They are in a very similar state to a person at the lowest depths of separation but not reprobate. To be reprobate a person has to have at first been aware of the influence of the divine nature. Then they had to have repeatedly rejected it until the point that God gives them over to the whims of their human nature.

So how does the innocence of a child mirror the reprobate state?

It mirrors this because the child also is unaffected by the influence of divine awareness. God will not impute sin on the child until there is an awakening of the awareness of his divine nature at which point, he will hold them accountable.

There are two ways this accountability is reached:
1. It occurs naturally through age.
2. Through the parents.

The parental method is God's chosen method as we see in Proverbs 22:6 admonishing parents to train up a child and to teach them his statutes in Deuteronomy 4:9,10.

Because children do not respond or acknowledgment the influence of His divine nature God expects the parent to act in the place of a conscience for the child. Remember that the conscience acts as an alarm system to let us know that we are in violation of the divine nature. It is for this reason that God charges the parent with the responsibility of priming the pump to stimulate the awakening of that child's will unto His divine nature. Parents achieve this through the use of tribulation. The tribulation used is in the form of rules, boundaries and regulations. What must be realized about a child at infancy is that self-desire is the only part of their human nature that has any real influence on their life in the early years. They have no self-dependence and are completely dependent on the parent. As they age their ability to depend on themselves will naturally increase. So, you see, that this dependence upon their parent is in place of a dependence on God. Infants are not even that aware of their own selves but have a greater awareness of their parents because they are so reliant upon them. However, all children are born with a great amount of self-desire. This is the part of human nature that dominates their will. They will cry when they want to be fed.

They will scream when they are not fed immediately. They will throw tantrums if they are denied their way and so on. This desire eclipses the desire of their parents quite often. Therefore, through punishment, conditioning and rules the parent must influence the will of the child to reject the influence of human nature. So, we see that tribulation helps to disrupt the influence of human nature and free the will from bondage so that it can oppose it. While we are using children as an example God also uses tribulation in our lives for this same reason. As a child ages they will be more influenced by self-awareness and self-dependence increasing the overall sway of human nature over their will. Parents must continue to establish boundaries to curtail that influence by instituting the child in the knowledge of God's existence and expectations. The most important is the example the child sees of the parents' will being yielded to God's divine nature and the subsequent impact that it has on their actions. These actions will accelerate the awakening of the age of accountability within the child. When the child yields to the will of their parents they are yielding to the will of God as we read in Ephesians 6:1-3. The way that a child responds to their parents is how they will likely respond to God when they reach the age of accountability. So God will not impute any sin on the child until they reach that point as we see in Ezekiel 18:20. In order to understand how we arrived in our fallen state and how God used tribulation in regards to it we are going to take a journey back to a time long ago.

The Fall of Lucifer

We understand that in the beginning God created the heavens and the earth, Genesis 1:1. We also know that God specifically made the earth to be inhabited, Isaiah 45:18. Sometime before the creation of earth we can assume that God created the spiritual beings. Out of all of those spiritual beings he created a being so unique that they stood out from all of the rest. We can also assume that this being was the greatest out of all the others. Nowhere in the bible will you find mention of any other spiritual being adorned as Lucifer, the light bearer. His body was covered in precious stones such as sardius, topaz, diamond, beryl, onyx, jasper, sapphire, emerald, carbuncle and gold, Ezekiel 28:13. Also within that passage it speaks of taberets and pipes being prepared within him. Aside from the meaning of his name he held titles such as son of the morning, Isaiah 14:12 and the anointed cherub that covereth, Ezekiel 28:14. There is no mention in the bible of another created spiritual being having such prestige. So, we can safely surmise that Lucifer indeed was a special being, created to fulfill very special purposes. One of those purposes was to rule the inhabited earth over whatever beings that preceded man. As unique as Lucifer was and as greatly God esteemed him, we know that his light was engulfed by the adversary, Satan. It is this transition that will give us another glimpse of why God uses tribulation in our lives. To discuss this, we first must understand how sin was born.

Origin of Sin

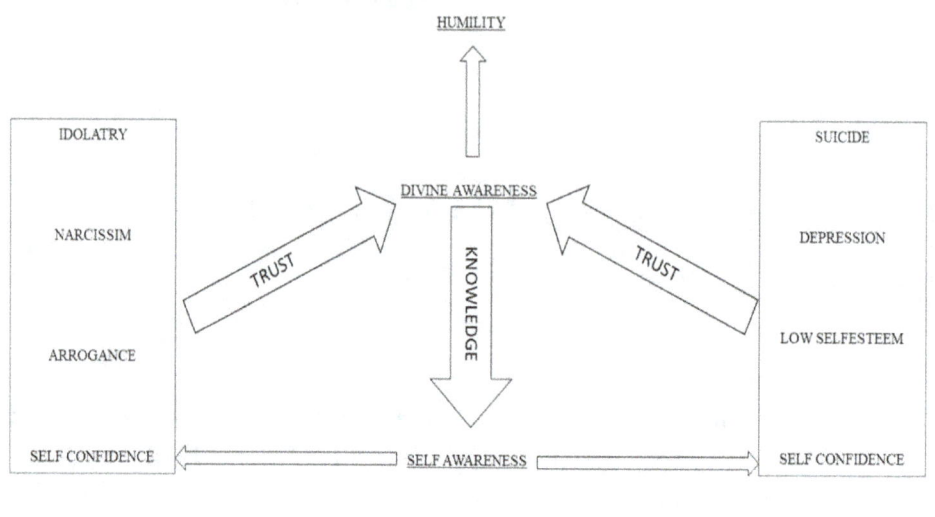

LEVELS OF PRIDE

As your self-confidence diminishes so does your faith in yourself. This is the point at which self-confidence gives way to low self-esteem. The more you doubt yourself and focus on what you can't do, you become unable to overcome your disposition. Doubt in yourself will grow exponentially and drag you into deeper levels of low self-esteem. Low self-esteem eventually gives way to depression. Neither low self-esteem or depression are sinful. However, at some point during your downward spiral, doubt will gradually erode your faith in God. We all deal with intermittent points of doubt, which really is a weakened faith. This is not sinful, and it is a natural, inevitable phenomenon of our spiritual walk. The further you descend into depression that doubt will be so frequent that it becomes a permanent way of thinking. During this descent you will begin to project your lack of capability onto God. Because you can't, God can't and your lack of belief in self becomes a lack of belief in God until you believe in neither yourself or God. It is during this transition that your depression, a lower level of low self-esteem, becomes sin. This is also where depression gives way to the flirtation of suicidal thoughts. The longer someone remains drowning in their lack of belief in self, God or anyone else, they reach the conclusion that there is no longer a reason to exist. So, the final stage of low self-esteem is suicide. Suicide is a completely selfish act that disregards God and others. This act is conducted due to the absolute disregard of a person's life to the extent that it is viewed to them as worthless. What makes this a prideful act is that all life was and is worth the life that Jesus sacrificed for it, expressing the true value of each individual life to God, read John 3:16. The important thing to realize with pride that is born out of low self-esteem, is that God does not resist it but rather reaches down to pull us up. What better illustration then the account of Peter when his focus shifted from Christ to his lack in himself to do the impossible that he was already doing, read Matthew 14: 27 - 31. Jesus did not stomp his head beneath the sea while scolding him for his fear and doubt. Keep in mind that this doubt arose from low self-esteem after he humbly stepped out to do the impossible, due to his trust in Jesus. The point is Jesus swiftly reached down to aide him, along with questioning his reason for leaning upon his own understanding.

On the other hand, as your self-confidence increases, so does your faith in yourself. This may seem to be a good thing, but it is quite the opposite. The reason is, as your faith in yourself increases, your faith in God decreases. Also, the more self-dependent you are the less you will look unto God or see a need of God for provision. This is where self-confidence gives way to arrogance. Arrogance is sinful pride and while at first you may still go through the motions of praise and prayer, your heart will be far from him, as we find in Matthew 15:8. It is for this reason that God will reject you, read Isaiah 1:2 - 15; 1 Peter 5:5. The more your faith in yourself grows and your faith in God diminishes, your self-admiration will grow. The more your adoration of self-increases the more focused you are on fulfilling your own desires. This is when arrogance reaches its next level, narcissism. Once you have become narcissistic, your love for God rapidly diminishes as self-desire eclipses divine desire, see 2 Timothy 3:2. All the desires of self are precedent, yet as seen in the scripture, an appearance of godliness can still be maintained.

Although, the more a person is given over to self-fulfillment they will no longer see a need for an appearance of godliness. Self will be all that matters, and fulfillment of self-desire the only pursuit. It is at this point that God will either be replaced with self or someone or something else. All knowledge, gain and achievement are now attributed to self, something else, or someone else read Daniel 4:29,30. This is the point at which narcissism gives way to idolatry. Notice the stark contrast in response by God to the upper levels of pride as seen in the account of Herod in Acts 12:21-23 and Nebuchadnezzar in Daniel 4:31-37. God will always bring low all who are lost to the ascension of the upper levels of pride, but it is still an act of mercy that he will cast us down. With this we are ready to witness the birth of sin and its disastrous results.

Trust in God is what leads us to divine awareness and divine awareness leads us into the initial stages of humility. Humility is a God based confidence as opposed to self-confidence. However, this confidence in God is also projected unto us also. The difference is that in humility we are confident in our ability because God is our enabler, so we faint not nor are we lifted up in pride. This is the humility that allowed David to proclaim boldly before Goliath in 1 Samuel 17:26,45-51. Humility provides us with confidence to overcome all things because it is through Christ that we are enabled as we find in Philippians 4:13.

The Rise of Satan

We know that Lucifer was created in perfection as it says in Ezekiel 28:15. This means that his initial disposition was to be in humility. He leaned upon the Lord and not himself.

So where does tribulation come into play in this?

Tribulation arose in the form of a trial. This trial was initiated the moment Lucifer's self-awareness began to shift away from divine awareness. The lust of the eyes through knowledge began his transition from humility to self-confidence. What needs to be understood is that self-confidence is not a sin but as we discussed, a lack of it gradually leads to sin when you are swallowed by doubt and it immediately leads to sin when you become arrogant. Remember, arrogance replaces faith in God with a faith in self, as we saw with Nebuchadnezzar. However, in Lucifer's case he took knowledge of how marvelous and wonderfully made he was and became arrogant. In his arrogance he was lost in the uniqueness of himself in comparison to all the other spiritual beings and creations. Proof of this was in God's first admonishment of him being lifted up by his beauty in Ezekiel 28:17. His arrogance caused him to be more self-dependent. The increase of his self-dependence diminished his divine dependence, he now leaned to his own understanding. The evidence of this was in God's second admonishment of his brightness corrupting his wisdom. We now see his arrogance giving way to narcissism. What we begin to witness is as Lucifer is caught up in arrogance, the gradual transformation of the Light bearer into the Adversary takes place.

As we shall see, the transformation is not yet complete. The trial for Lucifer was to choose between obedience to God or rejection of God. What needs to be understood is that at some point Lucifer began to obey God out of a sense of obligation, meaning it was just to fulfill a requirement or check the box. We will cover such obedience in more depth further along. The point is, when his spiritual nature was opposed to God's divine nature his true motivations for obedience was challenged. Tribulation forced Lucifer to prove if he obeyed God out of love or only out of obligation. Basically, if an alternate choice was presented, contrary to the divine nature, what would it prove? Jesus expressed that obedience was the proof of our love for him in John 14:15. We also know that God discerns our intentions as we read in Hebrews 4:12, so what motivates our obedience also matters to him.

We know that Lucifer was so in adoration of himself that self-desire infected and distorted his mind. Through yielding to the pride of life his transformation was complete. His light was completely snuffed out by Satan. Satan had reached the conclusion that there was no longer a need for God, he was fully dependent on himself and only his desires mattered. Therefore, he logically would become god and finally pride was in full culmination as idolatry. However, in his perverted mental state, being a god was not enough. In his mind God should be subject to him even as the earth and its inhabitants. We see proof of this in Isaiah 14:13,14. Not only did he rebel against God, but he deceived angels to join in his cause and they also took on a fallen nature. Revelations 12:4 speaks of the dragon's tail that cast a third of the stars to the earth referencing what Satan did to the angels that followed him. Revelations 12:9 speaks that during the time of his failed rebellion that he also deceived the world. In consideration of the frame in which I am placing things we will assume that Satan deceived the beings God gave him to rule on earth, poisoning them against God, like he did to the angels. God's response to such was to make the earth empty, and a waste as we read in Isaiah 24:1 and without form and void in Genesis 1:2.

Origin of Demons

I wish to provide conjecture on this mysterious subject for a moment. Some theologians believe the demons in the bible are disembodied souls from the destruction of the Earth's prior inhabitants under the reign of Lucifer. Whether they come from those inhabitants or not I would like to provide support for the idea that they are disembodied souls and not angels. The strongest biblical evidence against an angel being a demon lies in the fact that it is proved that, though being a spirit, they are capable of manifesting a physical body. Yes, this includes fallen angels also. The only biblical account of the physical manifestation of a fallen angel is when they had sexual relations with women in Genesis 6:1,2. We know that this unholy union created the abominations known as giants. Keep in mind that this was before the flood. During the flood God explicitly declared all land-dwelling life as perished: birds, men, reptiles, giants and etc... read Genesis 7:23. Just for emphasis, the passage ends stating that just Noah and those with him on the ark remained alive, with the exclusion of the aquatic life, of course. The reason for the emphasis is that we know sometime after the flood that the land of Canaan was populated with scattered groups of giants. This means fallen angels manifested in a physical body and repeated their sinful union. By Israel and other people God purged these abominations and cast those fallen angels into hell to be chained and await future judgment read Jude 6,2;2 Peter 2:4. Also we established that angels are able to manifest a physical body and do so to interact with man as seen with Abraham in Genesis 18:1-3 and after the resurrection of Christ in Luke 24:2-5.

The most fundamental characteristic the bible tells us about a soul is that it is created initially from God breathing a portion of his spirit into a physical body read Genesis 2:7. First of all, we have discussed that angels are spirits and don't possess a soul or a physical body even though they can manifest a physical form. Second, in order for a soul to interact with the physical realm it requires a physical body to do so. Before I continue, let me disqualify another candidate from the demon list, souls of wicked people. It is clear in the account of the rich man and the beggar that both righteous and wicked are immediately translated to their pre-judgment fate as seen in Luke 16:22,23. We also are admonished that we have once to live then we will be judged read Hebrews 9:27. While it is unclear in scripture as to who demons are or were, the evidence that they are disembodied souls is strong. The bible speaks of how they eagerly seek for a physical body to find rest read Matthew 12:43-45; Mark 5:12,13. We have already established the soul as the heart of an individual, their seat of emotion. This would also make the soul the seat of individual personality. So, each demon could be considered an individual personality.

Demon Possession

With that in mind, let us take a brief look at demon possession. We will categorize it into two distinct forms:

1. Domination.
2. Symbiotic.

Domination

This is characterized by instances where the demon is in full control of the host body read Mark 5:3-5; Matthew 17:15, 9:33, Acts 19:13-16, Luke 8:29. Another characteristic is the suppression of the host personality read Luke 8:30-32. When the host personality is suppressed the demonic personality or personalities speak in place of the host as we see in Legion's case as well in Acts 19:13-16 with the sons of Sceva.

Symbiotic

Unlike domination, there is a willful, mutual coexistence between the host and demonic occupant or occupants. As a result, the demon or demons grant supernatural attributes to its host in exchange for their cohabitation.

These are some of those granted attributes:

1. Sorcery - This is seen with Pharaoh's wizards who withstood Moses in Exodus 7:11,12,22, 8:7 and with Simon the sorcerer in Acts 8:9-11.

2. Divination - An example of such is seen with the witch at Endor in 1 Samuel 28:7,8.

3. Sooth saying or fortune telling - An example of such is seen in the account of the damsel that troubled Paul in Acts 16:16-18.

CHAPTER 5

The Fall of Man

Now we flash forward over hundreds of thousands or millions of years to a point where God stoops over the dust of the ground of a restored earth. With tender love and care he scoops up the dust and does something so unique that he had never done it before. Since the beginning such a thing had not been accomplished. That event was the creator of all things making something in his own likeness. This eclipses the splendor that once was Lucifer, setting this creation in much more esteem than anything else. God named this creation that manifest his likeness in a physical form man and gave them dominion over all the earth read Genesis 1:26.

Do you understand the significance of this?

Let's look at it like this:

1. God always intended for the earth to be ruled by a unique creation.
2. Aside from man only Lucifer was given such a highly distinguished body that clearly set him apart from other created beings.
3. Man was Lucifer's replacement to rule the earth.

I like to present a question to you that perhaps you have entertained.

Why did God test man in the garden?

I'm sure the thought has popped up before and while answers have been given by many a theologian, I'd like to provide my own conjecture.

Before I do, let's discuss some things. Just as Lucifer was created perfect in complete humility and fully confident in God to accomplish all things, so were both Adam and Eve. Before Eve was created God placed Adam in the garden to dress it and immediately told him how he could freely eat of every tree except the tree of the knowledge of good and evil read Genesis 2:15-17. Along with the command came the consequence for disobedience, death. Now consider that with Lucifer, he served God willfully but out of obligation only. The proof of that as well as the fallen angels and the earth's former inhabitants is, that when they were presented with a competing interest, they rejected God's divine nature. This rejection proved their love of self-desire was greater. So instead of allowing things to just run their course God desired to get his answer right away with man. God gave him a single command in order to do so. It is a good assumption that God had further responsibility, authority and prestige in store if Adam and Eve were to choose the divine nature over their human nature. God wanted to determine if man would serve him out of obligation or because they loved him.

How was God to go about proving their love?

The answer to that is through tribulation. Temptation would be the form in which that tribulation would come. God would not be the one tempting, God does not tempt nor can he be tempted. What that essentially means is, God does not coerce, beguile or seduce in order for his will to be carried out but he does test, which is also a form of temptation. What needs to be understood is that just because Adam and Eve were presented with a choice, which is also a form of tribulation, simply choosing to subject to God was not his sole desire.

We have learned two things about why God uses tribulation so far:

1. He does so to stimulate the use of our will to choose him.
2. He does so to prove our love for him.

After their creation we can assume that for a short duration they willfully fulfilled God's will. During this time, due to their humility, there likely existed some type of protective covering upon them. This covering along with other attributes helped to diminish the influence of human nature upon their will. In the pre-fallen state all of their human nature was fully subject unto the divine nature and in a sense, it could be considered dormant. After serving God and enjoying the goodness of the garden he provided one day Satan would come onto the scene and fully arouse that dormant nature. This would be the catalyst to put them in a position to truly exercise their free will. They would be forced to determine why they really obeyed God. For the first time they would have an equally competing interest to choose self-awareness or divine awareness, self-dependence or divine dependence and self-desire or divine desire. The result of such a choice would prove to God if they served him because they loved him. Anyone could serve because it is the right thing to do or what is supposed but that is no different than being a robot.

The Test

Before we look at Satan's deception let's discuss why he tempted them:

1. He was jealous that God had the audacity to make a being more unique than himself by creating man in his own image.
2. Because man looked like God he wanted to defile man.
3. He was angry that man replaced him as sovereign over the earth.
4. He desired to rule over man so that he would feel as if he ruled over God.

When Satan through the serpent addressed Eve and indirectly Adam, since he was with her, he appealed to every aspect of their human nature. The first appeal was to self-awareness through the pride of life. Notice the devil's argument about her eyes being opened, being as gods, knowing good and evil, seeing the tree as good for food read Genesis 3:5-6. At this point she shifted from humility through that acknowledgment of herself to self-confidence. It was about what she could obtain by her own ability. Divine awareness began to fade the more she realized herself. The next to be aroused was self-dependence by the lust of the flesh. By seeing that the fruit was pleasant, was an understanding of the fruit being able to be obtained by her own strength, its beauty and all it had to offer. Therefore, the light of divine dependence was neutralized as the will was dragged further into the depths of separation. The culmination of the process was with the awakening of self-desire through the lust of the eyes. At last she realized it was a tree desired to make one wise. The warmth of divine desire that opposed them eating from this one tree became neutralized as the will was dragged to the deeper depths of separation. At this point, Eve had become narcissistic, as well as Adam, for their love of self had eclipsed their love of God. This propelled her into her next realization which took her into a level of narcissism where her and Adam straddled the line between narcissism and idolatry. While there is no bold proclamation to overthrow God, the subjection of their will had already shifted away from the divine nature to human nature. Finally, she ate, gave it to Adam and he ate. Sin had now slain them.

In this fallen state, just as Lucifer's brightness went out, so did a light go out in man. In their perfect state there was a protective covering of innocence but now that was stripped away. The result was that they were ashamed of a nakedness they were well aware of but it was not originally viewed with shame read Genesis 2:25. Also they lost a natural peace of mind that covered them which gave way to fear, more so a fear of God read Genesis 3:10. Consider this, after their creation in their perfect state, no fear existed. There was no reason to fear him because they abode in righteousness, therefore God's wrath was not turned upon them. By abiding in his righteousness, they abode in his love. In God's perfect love fear is driven out read 1 John 4:18. While they remained in righteousness the fear they had of God was one of reverence, meaning because of his love that they reciprocated back to him, they had no desire to shame or hurt him by acting out against his will. Another reason was that in a righteous state their soul was in close proximity to the divine nature. When man rejected the divine nature that proximity changed on both sides. Isaiah 59:2 expresses that iniquity severs this closeness and God also rejects the individual as they willfully remain in that state. With the knowledge of this, the fear that drove them into hiding was terror, which had fully replaced their reverence. Terror was all they could feel at this point due to their rejection of the divine nature read Hebrews 10:26,27,31. So we see the reason for fear being manifest in fallen man. Physical nakedness was a manifestation of the loss of innocence. Genesis 3:9-11 shows that they hid from God because of their nakedness. In their narcissistic state there was no desire for repentance read Genesis 3:12,13. Due to this, wrath and judgment was all that they looked forward to, so they had no peace in meeting with God.

I want to point out something easily overlooked. Adam and Eve had free access to knowledge without being disobedient. We understand that all knowledge begins with God read Proverbs 1:7 and to obtain wisdom, during those cool walks in the garden all they had to do was ask and it would have been given liberally as we read in James 1:5. Therefore, it is a safe assumption that God would not have withheld anything from them that they asked. They were commanded not to eat of the fruit of the tree of the knowledge of good and evil. God never condemned them about obtaining the knowledge by asking. Death was a result of partaking of the fruit. The point, is that Satan offered them to obtain knowledge outside of divine dependence. He deceived by telling them God was wrong, that death would not come but the lure was gaining knowledge through self-dependence. Another thing is, Adam by not asserting his sovereignty that God gave him over all creatures, he yielded to sin and the master became a slave. First, man's soul was in captivity to human nature, which nullified much of the influence of the divine nature. We have discussed this in the depths of separation. The next thing to happen was man became subject to Satan, the master of human nature in fallen man. Jesus explained this to the rebellious Pharisees of who their father was in John 8:39-45 and Paul about those who walk according to the course of this world and fulfill the desires of the flesh in Ephesians 2:1-3.

Why did Adam and Eve still breathe after eating the fruit?

The answer is that God had a plan of redemption in place before he had created man. This plan included both the body and soul. This also sets man apart in that spiritual beings cannot be redeemed once they have fallen. As we know, innocent blood was shed to temporarily atone for their transgression until the day Jesus would offer himself for the world.

CHAPTER 6

A Closer Look

I would like to give you a different perspective of time in order to grasp how the images below will help us. While we understand that time is a unit of measurement it is also the thing being measured. In other words, time is synonymous with life. While we don't know the day the earth was created, the passing of years is measured before the birth of Christ and after his death. From January to December, by minutes, hours, days and months a year is measured, which equates to a fraction of the earth's life that has passed. So, it can be said that time is used to measure time. While it is popular to view time as linear, I propose to view it as cyclical. From this perspective your forward movement is your aging.

Cycles of Life

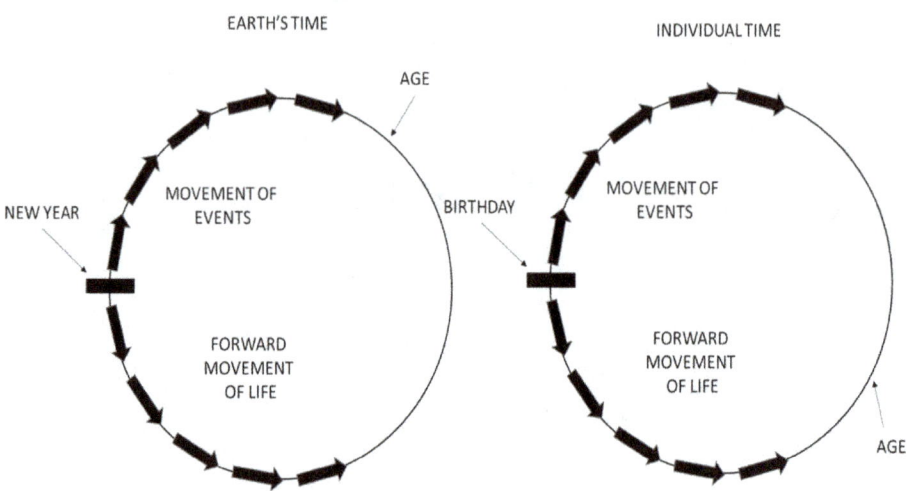

EARTH'S TIME

INDIVIDUAL TIME

AGE

NEW YEAR

MOVEMENT OF EVENTS

BIRTHDAY

MOVEMENT OF EVENTS

FORWARD MOVEMENT OF LIFE

FORWARD MOVEMENT OF LIFE

AGE

We measure the earth's time from new year to new year and our own from birthday to birthday. The minutes, hours, days, and months that pass in-between represent the forward movement of life, our aging. During that forward movement toward a new year or birthday events will take place. These events will range in-between pleasant and traumatic. Since the earth's time and an individual's time is synonymous, what happens to one will effect the other. We understand that seasonal natural events, holiday events and national events are reoccurring at specific points along the Forward Movement of Life (F.M.L.). It is for this reason the Movement of Events (M.O.E.) is depicted as moving counter to the F.M.L. So, you see that events can become Fixed Points of Experience (F.P.E.) that will be revisited in the future or present. What needs to be understood is that the more memorable the event is when it was experienced it may also become a F.P.E. This means events outside of natural occurring ones such as holidays and seasonal weather patterns can also become recurring.

This is seen more so in the individual time cyclic pattern. This also has more to do with traumatic events from the past. These traumatic events become Fixed Points of Experience that reoccur throughout the

Forward Movement of Life but can also become a Point of Immobility (P.O.I.). A Point of Immobility is an experience that keeps a person fixed in place even though they outwardly continue to age. Even though a person in this case will become older they are no longer truly moving forward, therefore there is no longer any forward movement due to the unmovable event. In either case whether the event is a F.P.E. or a P.O.I. they become hindrances. In order to simplify these hindrances, we will refer to them as doors. Before we go further, we need to discuss how these traumatic events become reoccurring. In a word, it has to do with suppression. Our body as an automatic defense mechanism, at times, will suppress memories of events that have greatly troubled us. This is not wholly to our benefit. The reason for that is, that the residual effects of the suppressed event will still play out in our physiology and in a psychosomatic way. What I am saying is, that past trauma can go unnoticed in the present and future but your future and present behavior can be a result of that trauma without your realization. This type of behavior is especially so when you encounter future or present circumstances that bear similarities to your past traumas. When this takes place, they become a trigger or stimulation of past reactions to that trauma. It could be as simple as a familiar smell, color, music or even gesture that triggers a negative response to the present stimuli. You may not even realize why you are responding in such a manner due to the suppression. At other times you may experience partial or total recall of the past traumatic event.

In the case of Fixed Points of Experience or Points of Immobility, they become either open or closed doors. Some familiar characteristics of doors is that they are generally visible, have locks, are opened with a key and deny or allow access. The other unique thing about doors is the one who owns them has the authority to open and shut them because they possess the key. The doors in the life of an individual are a little different because of suppression. Because of suppression the doors can be hidden and may be wide open, letting things in that plague an individual throughout their life. The hidden doors of this type are represented by those Fixed Points of Experience that we spoke about earlier.

Other doors are locked and impede the Forward Movement of Life and are represented by Points of Immobility. Keep in mind that a Point of Immobility is a Fixed Point of Experience but one so powerful that it stops you dead in your tracks. The difference is that a F.P.E is something that keeps reoccurring but does not prevent you from moving on with your life such as a mild phobia. Once again, when or if it becomes more dominant it will transform into a P.O.I.

So where are the keys to lock or open these doors?

The answer is the key to the future lies in the past. The you in the present is a culmination of your response to past events. So, to really understand yourself, you must go backward in order to move forward. This is why the key to the future lies in the past. The catalyst to send us into this backward investigative journey is tribulation. Because of suppression it takes us to undergo events of great significance to force us into a total recall. In this time of recall we are presented with the key to lock or close a door that is allowing hindrances in the present to beset us. Because of this, our will is influenced or motivated into action. The divine nature will impress upon us to do things such as forgive, tolerate, seek counsel or take measures to rectify the situation. This is especially so in cases where your Point of Immobility is a grudge. Bitterness is the fuel that sustains a grudge and aims it like a knocked arrow to loosen upon another for some wrong they did to you decades in the past. However, through yielding to the divine nature you will obtain the key to unlock this door and truly begin to move forward with your life. In this case that key is forgiveness of a Godly sort.

Forgiveness will have liberated you:

- Emotionally from the heavy weight bitterness has placed upon your heart.
- Physically from whatever ailments that are associated with it that plague your body.

On the other hand, human nature will impress upon the will to do whatever it takes to reject the recalled event. It is for this reason that denial is the first stage when we are presented with taking accountability for past events.

Other responses are:
- Fear.
- Resentment.
- Anger.

The result of the responses of human nature are the rejection of the recalled event and a throwing away of the key. This is what leaves a person stuck and makes it a Point of Immobility. When this happens, they will be continually plagued by the residual effects of this unresolved past trauma. Sometimes tribulation causes us to hit the proverbial rock bottom. In this state those suppressed events are also jostled loose and force us to have a partial or total recall. Either way the will is motivated into action.

It should be evident that with the absence of tribulation that:
- Hindrances from past events cannot be recognized.
- We will remain oblivious to why we are going through present trauma.
- We have no means to resolve our current problems.
- We become complacent in either being stuck or plagued by these doors.

An individual who rejects tribulation instead of allowing it to bring their will under the influence of the divine nature will, inevitably become stuck at a Point of Immobility. We need to realize that God's desire for tribulation is for it to be an asset and a tool. A tool that will aide us in breaking our will loose from the grip of human nature. During the tribulation experience the captive will is loosed from human nature. It frees the will long enough for the influence of the divine nature to be felt again. It is during that crucial time that God patiently awaits to see what we will do with our freedom. This is seen the most plainly throughout the book of Judges. This is also why there is an inherent aversion to change within the heart of mankind, especially change that goes against our human nature. Our human nature will do whatever it takes to keep our will under subjection. Even so, God will do or allow whatever it takes to deliver us from its grasp. However, his method is not something that we usually find the most pleasant, tribulation.

CHAPTER 7

The Tribulation Process
Part 1

We will use Romans 5: 3-5 to define the tribulation process. 3 And not only so, but we glory in tribulations also: knowing that tribulation worketh patience.

4 And patience, experience; and experience hope:

5 And hope maketh not ashamed; because the love of God is shed abroad in our hearts by the Holy Ghost which is given unto us.

So as a Christian we glory in tribulation because it works patience. Before we explain how patience is worked let's take a step back. We have already discussed that freeing the will from the bondage of human nature in order to motivate it into action is one of the purposes God uses tribulation for. The first action of tribulation in the believer is the brining of the will back unto humility. This is initiated when there is a shift away from self-awareness. Remember, knowledge is what begins the transition away from divine awareness unto self-awareness. We have learned that self-awareness gives way to self-confidence. Self-confidence gives us a greater inclination toward self-dependence. As we become more dependent upon ourselves it fuels our self-desire. With an increase in self desire a person may move into the upper levels of pride toward idolatry and replace God or into the lower levels of pride toward suicide and become so burdened with doubt that their faith in themselves and God is lost. At the end of either state the outcome is the same, God is rejected.

Therefore, tribulation is the catalyst to shift the will toward divine awareness. This shift is the first step toward humility. Tribulation sets this into motion by patience. Patience is a byproduct of our endurance of the tribulation experience. The spark of tribulation increases our divine awareness and our endurance of tribulation stimulates the will to lean toward divine dependence as opposed to self-dependence. This is defined best by Proverbs 3:5. By trusting in the Lord the will leans away from self-confidence while experiencing tribulation as human nature is denied. Now, we understand that the patience being worked by tribulation is actually our trust. This tells us that in order to achieve humility that we must trust in the Lord. Patience is the exercising of our will to yield to divine dependence and this leads to humility. Humility is best defined by Philippians 4:13 which says, "I can do all things through Christ which strengtheneth me." This shows us that the foundation or cornerstone of the tribulation process is the development of our trust in God.

Once again, divine awareness leads to humility which gives way to a greater divine dependence. In this state there is a shift away from self-desire as divine desire, which is what pleases God, becomes the central focus. The growth of that trust, driven by tribulation, leads to a hiding of his word in the heart, read Psalms 119:11, as well as a hunger and thirst for his righteousness, read Matthew 5:6. These things become the building material for the foundation that we mentioned. Our experience is the thing that is built upon this foundation. Therefore, this makes experience the structure being developed. This experience is best defined by Proverbs 3:6. By trusting in God as we endure tribulation, we witness his providence. Our trust is rewarded as he directs our path by his word, read Psalms 119:105. As his word directs us through the tribulation experience, we realize that our situation is working out for our benefit, read Romans 8:28. Humility is the capstone or finalization of this experience as we come to understand that through him we are enabled. In this understanding we realize that through him we are also more than conquerors, read Romans 8:37. If you pay close attention to this passage it explicitly states that in all of those things you are more than a conqueror but it is by the power of the one that loved us. So, in the midst of your nakedness, your distress, famine, peril, sword or persecution and tribulation you are not just a conqueror but more than a conqueror. Your conquering ability is derived from your humility. So, no matter what your senses say during those scenario's you must go back to allowing these situations to continually drive you to trust in the Lord rather than leaning upon your own understanding. Human nature will do its best to make you do otherwise, but our thoughts, feelings and perceptions do not negate the truth of God's word. Every doubt that arises through your nakedness, famine, sword and so on as you try to cling to a reality of being something that tangibly is impossible does not weaken the hand of God. Why? It is because it is through Christ that we can do and shall do all things, including being more than a conqueror in all of those situations. I want to stress that this is not after those situations have been resolved or God has provided a way or an answer but from start to finish and right in the very middle while you toil in prayer you are more than a conqueror through Christ. This is the experience that is being built upon that foundation of trust.

Therefore, from this experience hope is established. Remember that this is a result of remaining humble by trusting in him. That trust began with divine awareness giving way to a greater divine dependence and by you seeking to please him which is the yielding to divine desire. In this state hope is established by his love during our tribulation experience. Our hope is established as he shows us that nothing can stop him from loving us, read Romans 8:38,39. It is for this reason, that as we remain humble and trust in him that we will have no shame. We have no shame before him because we abide in righteousness. By remaining in righteousness, we abide in his love. By abiding in his love we are not ashamed because there is no fear in love, read 1 John 4:18. Not only is there no terror in his love but in this life we will not be ashamed before him when we see him, read Matthew 25:34.

So, from what has been discussed in this chapter as well as the others, you should have clear answers to the following questions that were presented in chapter 1:

1. Why does God allow us to suffer?
2. Why must we go through tribulation?
3. Is there something wrong with me if I have no joy in suffering?
4. Do we experience tribulation as a form of punishment?
5. Does tribulation mean God has forsaken me?

One thing that should be evident is the necessity of tribulation to achieve what we discussed in the tribulation process. This illustration below doesn't show us the complete picture of that process, but it is close. We will use it as a visual representation of the relationship of trust and tribulation in conjunction with the Christian archetypes.

The Tribulation Process

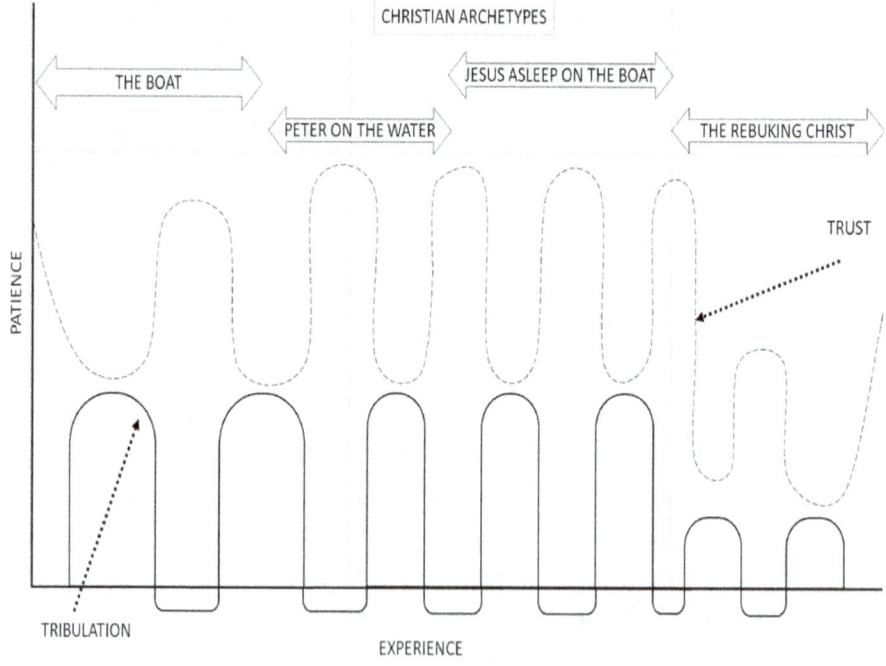

When the scripture explains to us that our strength is renewed by waiting on the Lord, it does not necessarily mean inactivity. It means more so, not anxiously acting based off of self-dependence but rather trusting in him. When we trust in God, we also have an expectation that God will move according to his word. So, you can say that trust and expectation is more so what it means to wait upon the Lord. When our will yields to divine awareness and divine dependence we shift away from self-confidence to humility. This is the point that we experience God's providence as we have discussed. In Mark 6:47-51 we find the disciples toiling against the winds as they tried to cross without Jesus. When Jesus met them on the sea and they let him in, the winds were calmed, and they reached their destination. As you see above, trust in God declines when we become self-confident. At this point we would transition from the boat archetype or Peter Walking on the water to the sinking Peter archetype as we are dragged into the depths of separation. Before we move on, let me clarify something. God does expect us to make our own decisions, so trust in him does not negate this. However, decisions made in humility are made with an inclination of the will toward divine awareness. An example of this is seen in Joshua 6 in the conquering of Jericho. Through trusting in the instruction of God Joshua lead Israel to victory. Decisions made out of self-confidence are made with an inclination of the will toward self-awareness. This is leaning to our own understanding. An example of this is seen in Joshua 7 and the defeat of Israel at Ai. Riding on the high of the previous victory, Israel shifted away from humility to self-confidence and saw no need to consult God in their battle plans. The result was defeat because victory over the enemy was promised through humility, trusting in God. So we see as trust declines, tribulation increases in our lives to cause us to ask, seek and knock as it speaks of in Matthew 7:7. We see just this type of humility from Joshua and Israel after their failure to take Ai and God helps them to realize what he would have shown them if they would have sought him in the first place. From this we realize again that tribulation is necessary to rock the boat and keep us aware of God so that we can choose to humble ourselves.

Our hope and experience in God are contingent upon our trust in God which is our patience. The greater our trust grows, the greater our experience and hope in him will grow also. As we understand from Romans 5:3, it is tribulation that begins this entire process. The illustration above depicts the relationship between patience and experience as a decline in trust gives way to a rise in tribulation. This figure is more so a general, visual representation to display the idea but does not convey specific uses of tribulation in our lives. I will explain one of those uses in a moment. We talked about how low self-esteem can become harmful pride born from self-confidence. It is really a decrease in confidence in self from an over fixation on what we are not able to do because of an exclusion of God. It along with depression leads to sin as our incapability translates into God being disabled to change our situation. This happens because we project our own weaknesses onto God, and this erodes our faith and willingness to pray. If we do pray, due to our distorted image of God, we don't really believe that he is able and our prayers are hindered, read Hebrews 11:6. In our low self-esteem or depression, when doubt increases our faith begins to wane. However, initially you will still believe that God is and that he rewards. Remember that faith equals belief and trust. In a deeper state of low self-esteem or depression, the onset of harmful pride, lies in the loss of our trust in God. Belief without trust lacks any diligence on our part. This is so because our doubt has drained all of our confidence in ourselves and we then project this also onto God. This is why we go through the motions of prayer, but we have an empty hope in God coming through. This could even be born out of not receiving a past answer that we expected. When there is no diligence because we have no trust, God will not grant our petitions, read James 1:6-8.

Gideon's Plight

Have no fear, for God has shown us in the account of Gideon how tribulation is the remedy to rekindle our trust and lead us back unto humility. We turn to Judges 6 and 7 to see how God's dealing with this man bring us much hope. It is important to realize that God was not only aware of the shortcomings of this man's character but out of all Israel he chose him as a judge for his flaws. On the other hand, Gideon's negative view of tribulation (Israel was just being punished by God and he had forsaken them as a result or else that would not be happening) represented Israel's view of themselves. It also represents our own viewpoint during tribulation at times. We see this in his response in Judges 6:13. I know that you may be thinking but they forsook God, however God never gave up on them. His blessing was based on the condition of their humility, trust, and obedience. Besides, listen to how God viewed Gideon, a mighty man of valor, read Judges 6:12 and go in his might, he would save and God had sent him, read Judges 6:14. What a stark contrast to his lack of confidence in himself due to low self-esteem, read Judges 6:15. Due to self-awareness his will was overtaken by low self-esteem and his poor view of self and lack of ability was projected onto God. But we see this encounter with God was tribulation in the form of a test. By God giving him this commission, his will was now motivated to go against his human nature and be lured to the divine nature by trusting in God's word. His willingness to do so is shown in seeking a sign, read Judges 6:17-19. Keep in mind that God was well aware of the weakness of this man's faith and did not condemn him for it but as he admonished through Paul in Romans 14:1, he received him. No this is not completely out of context. The proof is that Gideon did not lack faith, but he was not at the level of humility God desired. God was seeking a full divine awareness where Gideon leaned on God to the degree that his own capability or lack of ability did not matter. I will prove this as we continue. Instead of anger God accepted his request and began to goad his will closer to divine awareness where his self-dependence would yield to divine dependence. This was done through God accepting the offering at his hand, verifying his authenticity, read Judges 6:21-24. After this when he receives instruction in Judges 6:26 he does not hesitate to obey. Although, because of his lack of confidence he does so in a more comfortable manner, read Judges 6:27,28. Because of his trust in God and obedience, we see the increase in his humility as he experienced a greater peace, which came along with God directing his steps. We see this in his response to the retaliation of the Midianites and Amalekites gathering, which was to rally the troops. God's spirit came upon him as a result of his increasing faith, trust and humility as seen in Judges 6:34,35. Even so, Gideon had yet to reach the level of humility that God desired. Human nature would use fear to draw his will back unto self-awareness and self-dependence. Once more, he looks to his own incapability and questions God's ability to use one such as himself. Realize, God wanted him in such a state, which was brought on by the immensity of the gathering enemy force. God would show Gideon that it is not about his ability or the lack thereof, that he is able to deliver. Once more Gideon proves his faith and willingness to fulfill God's desire as we see in Judges 6:37-40. I'm out of my mind, right. Surely this is proof of a lack of faith, correct. Quite the opposite, I assure you. Gideon's will was inclined toward divine awareness but human nature through low self-esteem was tugging just as equally. We find the same situation with Jesus in the garden. Jesus was not afraid of the cross even though he despised the shame. Jesus came to go to the cross and did not avoid it. Neither was Gideon trying to avoid his task. In both instances' human nature fights for control of the will. It was so great an ordeal that Christ sweat blood as he wrestled in prayer three times. It was so great an ordeal with Gideon that he prayed twice. In both situations human nature was overcome.

Now that Gideon remained humble, aware of God, dependent on him and determined to fulfill his desire, God was going to build hope upon that experience.

So how does he do so?

Tribulation is the answer, in the form of a test, read Judges 7:2-8. Right on the precipice of victory human nature would seize hold upon his will and incline it back to his incapability. Once again, he was right where God wanted him. God did not chastise but instead encouraged him as we see in Judges 7:9-18. It was this final work that God brought Gideon's will into humility where it was wholly yielded to the divine nature. The result of this was not only victory over the enemy but freedom from the bondage of his low self-esteem.

CHAPTER 8

The Tribulation Process
Part 2

The Melting Pot

Through tribulation Gideon's faith was tried as gold in the fire like it speaks of in 1 Peter 1:7, for his edification and God's glory. The thing about gold is that it must undergo a certain degree of heat until the melting point is reached. Once this crucial point is reached, something special happens. It is then, that impurities are released from the metal. The name of these impurities is dross. The consistency of dross is lighter in weight than the gold and will rise into a filthy muck that floats on top. This dross is then removed and discarded. The longer the gold remains at its melting point the more dross is released. The more dross that is removed the more pure and valuable the gold becomes. God uses tribulation to bring us to the proverbial, melting point. He also uses it to keep us at this point. It is at this point that our will is motivated. Just as different metals have different melting points, so it is with people. God knows just how much tribulation it will take to bring certain issues to the surface. Then as it rises to our attention, we are placed in the position to yield our will to divine awareness unto humility. In this place we will follow God's direction as seen in Romans 8:14 and seek pastoral counsel, conventional counsel, or repent or forgive. Either way, God directs us to deal with the removal of the dross and doing so makes us subject unto him. Although if we decide to yield our will to self-awareness unto self-confidence when we reach the melting point, things will be very different. Remember, that the more self-confident we become the less we will trust God. The result of this is a greater self-dependence. It is from there we become either arrogant or drop into low self-esteem. Whatever rises to the surface and is addressed by arrogance, will convince us that we can handle it. In this thought pattern it is easy to deny the reality of the addictions that we have become enslaved by. When it is addressed with low self-esteem, we become gradually depressed. Also, our faith is slowly eroded by doubt as we eventually project this weakness onto God. We have already discussed the fatal results of this thought pattern. This results in God not granting our petitions. Even though we are lacking in diligence God is not. So, in response to our great weakness God's love will prove greater. God through the Holy Ghost will heat that furnace seven times hotter to purge us of the harmful dross of doubt. One method he will use is our fellow brothers and sisters in Christ. He will use them to help us to stop having pity on ourselves so that we can face these things and have the chance to choose humility. God also uses the world and pastors and so on to accomplish this.

In Our Weakness

As we mature in Christ God uses tribulation to help us remain in humility. This is especially so the more greatly that he uses us. Sometimes this type of tribulation comes in the form of infirmity. For such an example we look to what Paul expressed in 2 Corinthians 12:6-10. Paul was in such proximity to God that without the infirmity or some kind of ongoing tribulation his will would be more vulnerable to his human nature through complacency. The closer that we get to God the more of his peace we experience. The problem is that we remain in unconverted flesh and without tribulation to motivate the will, inactivity will gradually give way to self-confidence and arrogance or its opposite.

It is for this reason that one of God's greatest concerns with Israel before they entered the Promise land was them becoming complacent, which we find in Deuteronomy 6:10-19. He would overthrow and conquer their enemies through them and give them freely what they had not obtained by their own merit. As we know from Judges it was not long after their conquests began that their will shifted away from divine awareness unto self-awareness, thus they became idolatrous, replacing and rejecting God. We also know that this resulted in tribulation by judgment, which God by Moses forewarned would be the outcome for not keeping the covenant that they had made with him. We have another example in the heathen, Babylonian king Nebuchadnezzar. By God he conquered the world and became great as it states in Daniel 2:36-38. In the process of time his will was captivated by his human nature leading him from humility to Narcissism, read Daniel 4:29,30. No longer was it by God but by himself he obtained his glory and stature.

So how does God rectify this and free his will from bondage?

He does so by tribulation in the form of suffering, read Daniel 4:31-33. God's decree was not to harm this man for destruction, judgment yes but also to redeem him. This was his melting point to draw his will toward a divine awareness and humility, as we see was accomplished in Daniel 4:34-37.

So, in the example of Paul we realize that, at times our infirmities will not be removed. If God does not remove it, he sees it as a necessity in our mature state to keep us humble. This means that he wants our will to be yielded to divine awareness and remain dependent on him. The last thing he seeks is for us to be willing to fulfill his desire. Aside from doing so to keep us humble there may be other reasons that God does not remove our infirmities but in the end his ways are higher than ours and his thoughts than our own.

Most importantly if we pray and God doesn't take away our thorn, we should change our supplication. Sometimes we try to persuade God of the reasons why he should do so as Hezekiah in Isaiah 38:2,3 when we get no response. If we have gone a good while without an answer it is time to take another approach. An approach such as petitioning for God to use us just as we are. Ask him to show you how this infirmity can be used for his glory if he seems fit to leave you as you are. The point is, at times we ask and don't receive as it tells us in James 4:3 but it is not always because of our lust. In these cases, it is a matter as Paul's example clearly shows, that it is not denial by God but a matter of our will and his will being contrary. We also saw this when Paul was held back from going into Asia. His desire to take the gospel there was not wrong but it was not God's desire for him to do so. Paul had a heart for Asia and then Bithynia, but God's desire was for him to go into Macedonia as we find in Acts 16:6-10. So even though we may ask, it may not be for the right thing. When we seek, it may be in the wrong place. Also, when we knock, it may be on the wrong door. One example of seeking in the wrong place is 1 Kings 19:9. It was Elijah's fear that lead him to this cave, God had brought him to the mountain top and gave him victory. The point is that God does answer prayer.

However, these are his conditions when he does:

- Faith.
- Persistence.
- Diligence.

Faith

In Hebrews 11:1 the first thing it tells us about faith, is that it is the substance of things hoped for. In other words, the first part of faith is belief. The rest of the scripture says that it is the evidence of things not seen. So, the second part of faith is trust. The initiation of our faith is belief and that belief is thereby proved by our trust. The tangible substance of faith in which our belief is placed is experience. This experience is both other people's as well as our own. The proof of our own experience is in Romans 1:19,20. We believe God's word because it is his but also because it is reinforced through the truth that we experience with our senses. Then we also have past examples from the Old and New Testaments. These examples are reinforced as we respond with like faith, obedience or a lack there of, under similar conditions. So, you could say that as our trust in God increases, so does our belief. Remember, belief alone does not equate to faith, the demons also believe and tremble as it says in James 2:19. Faith will give way to obedience and obedience is the proof of our faith. Therefore, we can conclude that faith is derived of belief and trust.

Persistence

Our first example of persistence is found in Luke 11:5-8. Verse 8 reads, I say unto you, though he will not rise and give him, because he is his friend, yet because of his importunity he will rise and give him as many as he needeth. We find the second example in Luke 18:1-5. Verses 4 and 5 read And he would not for a while: but afterward he said within himself, Though I fear not God, nor regard man; Yet because this widow troubleth me, I will avenge her, lest by her continual coming she weary me. Persistence is pursuing our goals and desires without giving up, regardless of failure and denial.

Diligence

Our examples of diligence also involve persistence. Diligence is the manner of how we persist, which is with fervent determination. In Luke 15:8 it reads, Either what woman having ten pieces of silver, if she lose one piece, doth not light a candle, and sweep the house, and seek diligently till she find it? A similar event is in Luke 15:4,5 reads, What man of you, having an hundred sheep, if he lose one of them, doth not leave the ninety and nine in the wilderness, and go after that which is lost, until he find it?

So often in the case of infirmity we approach God with great faith and are persistent in prayer but what about diligence. We are quick to become deterred when we ask and get no answer, seek and don't find and knock but get no reply. Do you think that the woman quit searching for that silver piece because it was not found in the kitchen? Of course not, she moved from room to room looking in every nook and cranny until she found it, with great desperation, determination, and fervor. Jesus posed this question in Luke 18:8, will he find faith on earth when he comes. This was after he proclaimed that, God would avenge his elect though he bear long with them, Luke 18:7. Are you diligent enough to change your approach in supplication until your desire and God's are in alignment? Are you still willing to do so if you receive an answer that you did not petition for? Don't worry if you are not but realize that this is where tribulation is necessary. It is necessary so that we can be brought unto humility so that our true needs are met. In the end God is trying to get us to realize that Christ is all that we need. In other words, we our whole, perfect and lacking nothing, in Christ. You may be thinking, why and you can just fill in the blank that follows. The why, is because of our unconverted flesh and its susceptibility to our human nature. It is our human nature that interferes with the reality that in Jesus we are complete. As a result, it draws us back into bondage and changes that truth into a lie. It is for this reason that while we remain in this body, that we must undergo tribulation. The more we apply our faith, which hinges on our trust in God and is built upon our patience in God, that we will experience the truth of being whole in Christ. It is that experience that establishes our hope. Once again, all we need is Christ as it is through him that we can do all things and through him that we are strengthened, read Philippians 4:13. Also it is through him that loved us that we are more than conquerors in the midst of tribulations, distress, persecution, famine, nakedness, peril and sword. That him that loved us, is Jesus Christ, who by God's will gave himself as a sacrifice for the sins of the world as we see in John 3:16. Yes, God so loved the world that he gave but it was by the free submission of his will that Jesus obeyed the Father and offered his life as a gift to the world as we find in John 10:18. As we have learned this is the embodiment of the humility that God seeks in us through tribulation.

To Lift Him Up

Jesus had said that if he was lifted up that he would draw all men unto himself, read John 12:32. Consider this before I go further, that it was not until Jesus was brutally torn asunder and bleeding, hanging naked upon the cross and finally gave up the ghost that it would be fully realized, exactly who he was, read Mark 15:39.

What is the significance of this?

The significance is that it was in his greatest moment of suffering and subsequent death that the world was able to be reconciled unto him as well as realize who he was. It is also for this same reason that God allows tribulation to take place in our lives. So often we fall into the deceptive thought process that it is all about us. How could God allow this to happen to us and why doesn't he hear me. However, at times he allows for these things in our lives so that he may be glorified in the lives of others as they behold our suffering, just like Christ. What I am saying is, that in order for some people to come to know the reality of God they must first see Christ lifted up in our lives as we endure tribulation. It was when the blood of the martyr Stephen spilled upon the ground that day that the heart of the man Saul would be pricked. This would be the crowning event in his life that would shake loose his will from the grasp of human nature and draw it unto divine awareness. Many times Paul would recount that gruesome day as he does in Acts 22:20. The memory of Stephen as he boldly proclaimed for God not to charge their sin against them, would be an indelible blot upon the heart of Saul preparing him for the day he would finally yield wholly to the divine nature, read Acts 7:60. The witnessing of Stephen's death was the final straw to break Saul's will or draw it away from the bondage of his human nature. In another account we read of three young men who had to endure the flames of a furnace heated seven times hotter in order for a heathen king to realize who the true God was. Read Daniel 3:15-30. God not only allowed them to be thrown into the fire, but he joined them in the midst. Notice that the men who tossed them into the furnace died instantly. But we understand that it was not until Nebuchadnezzar had witnessed them endure the flames by boldly trusting in their Lord even at the threat of instant death, that he saw Jesus high and lifted up, read Daniel 3:28 -30. And finally for Isaiah to see the Lord properly in his life it took for the passing of king Uzziah as we read in Isaiah 6:1. Therefore as we humble ourselves and trust in the Lord as we suffer, God will draw others to him as they see his power at work in us, keeping the hunger of the flames from consuming us.

Cycle of Christian Growth

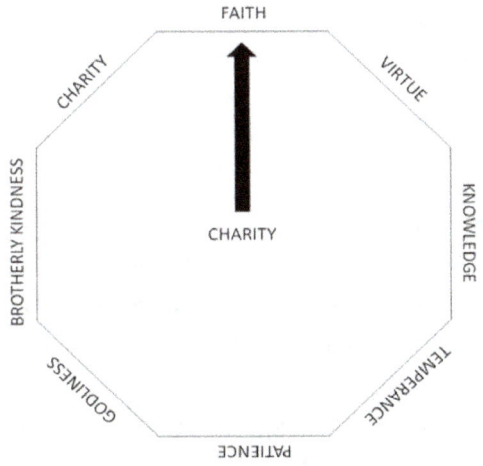

The goodness of God that leads us to repentance is the gospel message. His goodness teaches us of our sinful state that violates our creator. This understanding instills the fear of God in us and gives us the knowledge that we are accountable unto him. Because of the knowledge of that accountability, our will is motivated into action. The gospel also gives us hope. That hope is of the remedy provided by this loving creator, whose mercy rejoiceth against judgment as it says in James 2:13. Upon hearing of his charity, we receive the faith to be saved. This is why charity is the start of the cycle as we read in 1 John 4:19. We act upon our belief by trusting in his love which is shown by our repentance and subsequent salvation. The indwelling of the Holy Ghost attributes the virtue of God to us through Christ as we read in 2 Corinthians 5:21. Now, we have established our default status as a babe in Christ. However, by the indwelling of the Holy Ghost we are given basic, startup equipment. The first piece of equipment that we receive is knowledge which is gained by the initial fear of the Lord from hearing the gospel. Proverbs 1:7 makes this clear, that God is the source of all knowledge.

The remainder of our equipment is from the fruit of the Spirit as we find in Galatians 5:22,23:

- Love
- Joy
- Peace
- Long suffering
- Gentleness
- Goodness
- Faith
- Meekness
- Temperance

Keep this in mind, if equipment is not actively used for its intended purpose, it does you no good. It makes no sense to have something equipped if it is not being actively put to use. This begs us to ask a very important question.

What is the purpose for this equipment?

The answer is that it is there to aide us in our growth and keep us from being overcome by our human nature and taken back into bondage as is explained in 2 Peter 1:8-10. Even though we have a portion of what Peter is admonishing us to add, he is really speaking of two things.

Those things are:

1. You must actively apply your equipment to progress in your Christian growth.
2. You must actively maintain your equipment to perpetuate Christian growth.

The point is, that you already have what you need to grow as a Christian upon salvation. You also already possess the ability to maintain it. The problem is that these things are not activated autonomously as we read in James 2:14-20. That's right, God commands that we manually put these things into practice which we find in Philippians 2:12 and Ephesians 5:15-17.

Remember that as a babe in Christ, virtue was added when we received salvation. We are admonished to add it to faith as a warning to maintain the righteousness that we have acquired by faith. Even though we are converted, when we become complacent our will is heavily influenced by our human nature. If our will yields to that influence, we will be drawn back into bondage. Once this happens, we lose our virtue and our faith is lost as our soul becomes dead in trespasses and sin. There is no such thing as once saved always saved. Our virtue must be kept by the application of our equipment and the maintaining of our growth. Our growth is not some eight-step program, but it is a natural, sensible progression of attributes that give way to each other.

We have established that charity, God's love, naturally gives way to our faith in him. This is a natural and logical response to the reciprocation of that love. It is a response of the love that we received from Him and is given back to Him from us. The result of him receiving His love back from us is our reception of salvation from him. The receipt of that salvation is what results in His virtue being attributed to us.

Does this make sense?

Once again, we are back at square one, faith, but we are also moving through that natural, sensible progression. To keep our virtue, if that seed has fallen on good soil, we will be naturally inclined to do some things.

Those things are:
1. Hide his word in your heart, read Psalms 119:11.
2. Hunger and thirst for righteousness, read Matthew 5:6.
3. Allow his word to be a lamp, read Psalms 119:105.
4. Study to show thyself approved, read 2 Timothy 2:15.

As I have expressed, God will not need to constantly be on you. God will not need to be on you because it won't be a burdensome task as you will delight in is law like we read in Psalms 1:2. Even though you will have occasional battles with your human nature, more often than naught you will find that his word will be your desire. This attitude enables you to maintain your virtue by knowledge. The study of the bible, hiding of it in your heart, hungering for righteousness and allowing it to illuminate your way is the means by which you add or apply knowledge. It is through knowledge that we understand what the works of the flesh are as seen in Galatians 5:19-21. That knowledge also shows us the motivations of human nature that lead to those works of the flesh as is explained in 1 John 2:16. Finally by knowledge we learn how our will is influenced into yielding to these works and their motivations which is laid out in James 1:14,15. By knowledge we understand that unless we apply temperance, that the loss of our virtue will be in jeopardy. However, temperance also teaches us that in our anxiousness that we must not be in haste to act as is explained in Romans 12:19-21, Isaiah 40:31 and Proverbs 3:5-8. So, temperance logically and naturally gives way to patience, which is trusting in God rather than acting on impulse. As we learned with the levels of pride, trusting in God is the point that we begin to transition away from self-awareness and begin to move toward divine awareness. This transition not only leads us to humility but also to godliness. Godliness is divine awareness. Humility, as we grow and remain in it, will lead us to grow in our dependence on God. The more we depend on God, the more we will desire to please him. This leads to love-based obedience. As we remain obedient, we will fulfill his desire as we read in 1 John 4:16-21. We see then that godliness logically and naturally gives way to brotherly kindness. In turn, brotherly kindness is proof that we have charity and it naturally and logically gives way to it.

Does this mean we have now ended our growth?

Absolutely not.

The reason for this is so:

1. As long as we remain in our unconverted body, human nature will continue to vie for the control of our will to draw our soul back into bondage.
2. Because of the above we must actively maintain our growth.
3. Our growth is perpetual and ascending until death or the rapture.
4. We will become complacent at some point as it is our natural habit to do so when we receive greater blessings from God. Remember this is a result of our unconverted body.

Due to the above, for us to maintain our growth we must carry out the two greatest commandments. We do this by loving God with all of our heart, soul, mind, and strength along with loving your neighbor as yourself as it reads in Mark 12:29-31. It is upon these two commandments that hang, all the law and the prophets as we are told in Matthew 22:40. We also are told that love fulfills the law and works no ill toward his neighbor in Romans 13:10. In 1 John 5:2-5 it tells us that if we love God, we will keep his commandments. It is by the keeping of his commandments that we overcome the world as the end of verse four reads. The way we overcome is by our faith which we receive as a result of his love which is charity. Now we have come full circle, but the cycle continues as we grow stronger in these attributes.

So that's it right.

Absolutely not.

Things don't naturally progress that smoothly, even when we put our best foot forward. Our progress is hindered by our human nature. We also have the spiritual forces that join with that nature to use the natural affections of our body to seize our will and we will fail, repeatedly. We will also get discouraged, complacent, puffed up with knowledge and as Peter warned we will begin to lack in one or many of these. This is where God gets involved with the maintenance process through tribulation. As we discussed, trust is the key to leading us unto divine awareness and humility. Trust also is the proof of our love of God. While we are given patience upon salvation, only one thing helps us maintain it, tribulation. It is tribulation that works patience or motivates the will from the complacency of human nature as seen in Romans 5:3, James 1:3;1 Peter 1:5-7. Remember that faith equals belief and trust. That means that without tribulation it is impossible to reach our full growth potential in God. The reason is, that we must prove to God that no matter what we endure or for how long we endure it that we will choose to trust in him explicitly. This is done by the exercising of that faith we received by his love from his goodness that lead us to repentance. The result of this is his great and precious promises being realized as we are told in 2 Peter 1:4. Promises that we will receive in this life and in the life to come.

CHAPTER 10

Why He Suffered
Part 1

When we read 1 Peter 4:12,13,2:21, Acts 3:18 and Romans 8:17 we realize that suffering was an integral component for Christ. After reading Hebrews 5:7-9 the reason becomes clear, 7 Who in the days of his flesh, when he had offered up prayers and supplications with strong crying and tears unto him that was able to save him from death, and was heard in that he feared; 8 Though he were a Son, yet learned he obedience by the things which he suffered; 9 And being made perfect, he became the author of eternal salvation unto all them that obey him.

So, the result of Christ's suffering was him learning obedience.

With that said, lets address the following:

1. What is obedience?
2. Why did Christ need to learn it?
3. How did he suffer?

Obedience

We discussed that faith equals belief and trust. The evidence or authenticity of our faith is expressed by our obedience. In other words, obedience is the proof of our faith. It is proof and the completion of the trust that we place in God. It is easy to trust God when things are going smoothly but to obey no matter what, is the absolute proof of it. What needs to be understood is that there are two types of obedience but there are four different motivating factors behind them.

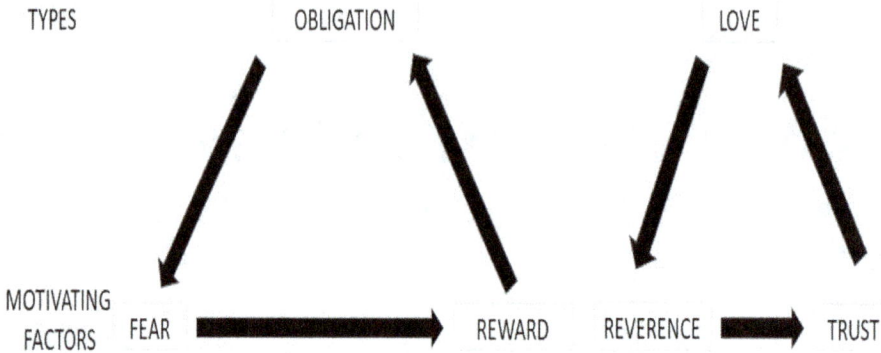

Obedience due to obligation is either done so out of fear or out of expectation of a reward. First of all, understand that neither motivation for obeying God is wrong but they will inevitably lead to sin if they remain the sole factors for obedience. The reason for this will be explained. As we know, through the receipt of hearing the gospel our faith is established as we read in Romans 10:17. It is by this faith that our divine awareness is kindled. As a sinner, through divine awareness we have a proper view of ourselves as Isaiah did in Isaiah 6:5. Proverbs 1:7 teaches us that this fear is the foundation of wisdom in our lives. This knowledge helps us to realize that it is a fearful thing to fall into the hands of the living God as we read in Hebrews 10:31. It also teaches us that the soul who abides in sin shall die as we read in Ezekiel 18:20,24-26. We also learn that the pay out of sin is also death and ultimately a definite judgment which is explained in Hebrews 9:27. Therefore, the gospel causes tribulation through this fear and stirs the will into a position of acting. The proper action is that we are obliged to serve God by accepting Christ so that we can appease his wrath and avoid judgment. Although, this form of fear is terror, it is used to shake the will free from the grip of human nature. We also know that the goodness of God leads to repentance as seen in Romans 2:4. Terror of his wrath helps us to realize that we need repentance in our sinful state. That same terror also helps us to realize as a saint that his goodness is not to be taken lightly. But we know as 1 John 4:18 tells us, that perfect love drives away terror. That means that terror will or should become fear out of reverence.

In a healthy spiritual progression, terror will give way to reward or a seeking to receive his favor or blessing. Once terror has revealed our need of repentance, the goodness that leads us to the altar is the gospel message itself as we see in these verses, John 3:16,17 and 2 Corinthians 5:17,21. The culmination is 2 Corinthians 5:21, For he hath made him to be sin for us, who knew no sin; that we might be made the righteousness of God in him. Due to the gain of everlasting life, righteousness, being made a new creature and avoiding his wrath and judgment, we are obliged to yield to his will. Because he first loved us, we fall in love with him as we are told in 1 John 4:19. This love of God, not the terror of God, is what draws us away from self-dependence to divine dependence unto salvation. Our love in response to his is what draws us away from self-desire unto divine desire at which point we have achieved humility.

What needs to be understood is that humility must be maintained, and the genuine nature of our love must be proved.

In the Greek they speak of three distinct types of love:

- **Eros** - a base type of love focused on desire, such as for sex, pleasure, food and sleep.
- **Phileo** - this is a brotherly love that is expressed toward family, friends and kindred spirits.
- **Agape**- is the highest form of love, a Godly and charitable love that is given without expectation and does so regardless if it is not reciprocated.

Because of what God has done for us we yield to his will and are obliged to please him. We continue in our walk from salvation by trusting God. The more we trust him the more we will obey him and as we obey him our love is proved to him. Trust is the key to love-based obedience. Only one type of love will keep you remaining obedient and it is borne from trust. That is the agape love, which is the love God is seeking and trying to develop in us. Trust motivated obedience leads us to a reverence type of fear that is focused on not shaming God rather than the terror of his judgment. Also, this yields a desire in us to be rewarded by feeling God's peace, presence and joy as opposed to a physical reward. Solely obeying for gain or out of fear of judgment does not yield to obedience out of love. Only by trusting God can we develop the proper motivating factors that lead to a charitable, sacrificial love, which is agape. In order for the genuine nature of our love to be proved, tribulation is necessary. Without tribulation to stimulate the will to act, there is no way to prove our love to God. What is proved, is the type of love that we really have, which pivots between the influence of self-desire and divine desire upon our will. Even when we are aware of God and choose to depend on God, the proof lies in what desire that we yield to when it is all said and done. As it has been said, "The road to hell is paved with good intentions."

What I am trying to express is that salvation is a progressive work until we die. During that progression human nature will impose upon our will through the affections of the body to draw our soul back into bondage. As the will becomes more inclined toward our human nature, starting with self-awareness, our motivations for obedience will begin to shift. Our motivations will shift away from a trust-based dominance to a reward, fear, or obligation-based dominance. The point is that the more these drive obedience, then the more diminished our trust will become. As our trust diminishes then so will our love for God diminish until we cease to love him any longer.

Consider these things:

1. Obedience dominated by terror, which is a fear of consequence and judgment, is short lived and really doesn't lead to love. James 2:19 tells us that even the devils fear God with trembling. When commanded they yield to God, but they do not trust or love him. As for man, terror will give way to eventual rebellion and rejection and at times resentment.

2. Obedience solely out of reward is done so with an Eros love. As long as duty is met with what is considered worthwhile, then service will continue. Jesus in John 6:26 rebuked the multitude for such, telling them they followed him for what they could gain. Another problem with this, is when God delays or seems to be withholding, this will lead to desertion. Satan duped Adam and Eve with the lie that God withheld knowledge from them, and they rebelled, proving at some point that their love shifted away from Agape to Eros. Since what they desired could be gained without yielding to God and he was not going to comply, they chose to desert him. Satan accused Job of serving God solely out of reward and challenged God on it, but we know that trust was his motivation, unlike Adam and Eve.

3. Obedience solely out of duty is done so with more of a Phileo love. It is driven by works with an appearance of godliness. Basically, one becomes religious and though the works are there, the heart becomes absent as we read in Matthew 15:8. The condition of the heart as the work is being done means more to God as is explained in 1 Samuel 15:22. This was Israel's greatest failure concerning the law, obedience became solely obligatory.

Therefore, in order to determine the motivations of our obedience as well as establish our trust, God utilizes tribulation. It is as we suffer that the genuine nature of our love is proved, based on the trust that we have shown God throughout our trial. Our trust is built as we place it in God while we are tried, and our obedience proves our love for him. Remember, that the necessity of tribulation is due to the continual influence of human nature on the will as it tries to coax it away from the influence of the divine nature. Without tribulation we will gradually grow complacent, which is the perpetual state the body desires to remain in. In our fallen state such rest leads to eventual bondage. God also desires a perpetual rest for the body but in an incorruptible vessel that we must prove ourselves worthy, in order to obtain it.

We know from the earthly life of Christ that trust was his continual motivating factor for a love-based obedience. As our forerunner of salvation, he showed us that trusting God and obeying out of an Agape love is the way to the heart of God.

CHAPTER 11

Why He Suffered
Part 2

His Lesson

Prior to leaving heaven, Christ did not require any lesson in obedience. The first clue to grasp this lies in why he left heaven. It is explained in Romans 5:12-14 that by one-man sin entered the world and brought God's wrath and death upon all men. Because of this Romans 5:15-19 tells us God decided that by one man, his grace would be issued unto salvation upon all men. The problem was due to the fall of man that their natural disposition was to be in bondage to human nature. It is for this reason that Christ could not enter the world by means of a natural conception. That is why it says in Hebrews 10:5 that a special body was prepared in the womb of Mary. Let's step back to the Spheres of Influence in order to discuss this vessel and its significance in Christ learning obedience.

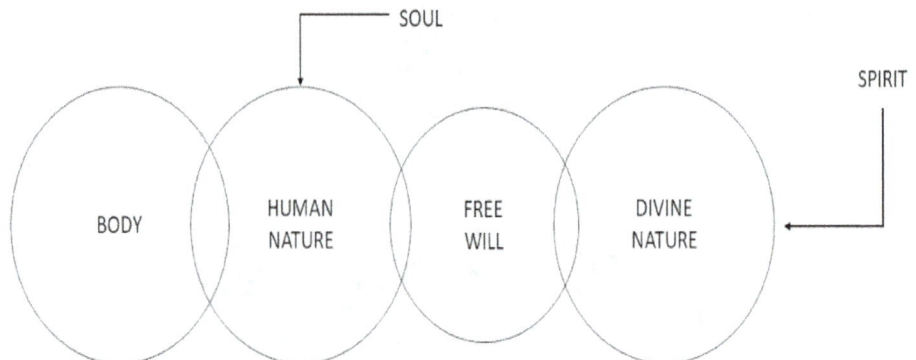

Spirit

Unlike all other creations who possess only a fragment of the divine nature, Christ as God possessed a full divine nature. This means that in this vessel there existed a full divine awareness, divine dependence and divine desire. The first proof of this is found in John 1:1-3 which tells us that the Word was in the beginning, was with God, was God and made all things. Hebrews 1:2,3, 8-10 not only says similar of the Son of God but explains that he is God. Finally, in John 1:10 we learn that this same Word not only was in the world but as John 1:14 states was also made flesh and dwelt among us. In other words, it is a safe assumption that at every phase of development in the womb that Jesus was aware of the fullness of his deity.

Soul

Just like Adam's soul after the creation of his body was alive without corruption, so it was for the soul of Christ, that dwelt within his physical body. And as Adam's soul was susceptible to the influence of human nature, so was the soul of Christ, susceptible to the influence of human nature. That nature consisted of a self-awareness, self-dependence, and self-desire. Remember that human nature is easily influenced by the whims and affections of the body.

Do you realize the significance of this?

The significance is that for the first time in eternity the unheard of and utterly impossible came to pass. We are admonished that God can't be tempted in James 1:13 but James 1:14 tells us that man can be tempted. Christ was both full God and full man encapsulated into one vessel.

So how was it possible for God to be tempted?

Will

Remember, as goes the will so goes the soul. The will is the bridge that both the divine nature and the human nature use to influence the soul. So, the reason that it was possible for God to be tempted was because God now possessed a soul. God possessed a soul that was subject unto human nature just like us. This means that it was possible for him to yield to that nature just as we do. The evidence of this is seen when Satan approached Jesus in the wilderness in Matthew 4:1-11. It was for this very reason that Satan tempted Christ and appealed to every aspect of his human nature just as he did unto Adam and Eve and succeeded. Unlike them, we know that Christ yielded to the divine nature and was successful where they failed. It is because of this vulnerability of the soul that Christ possessed, that it is said that our High Priest is able to have empathy with us because he was tempted in all points as we are which is explained in Hebrews 4:15.

Body

Just like Adam's body after creation was perfect and without corruption, so was Christ's. We also know that this uncorrupted state alone did not prevent Adam from allowing his will to be enticed by the natural affections of the body. We need to understand that the naturally occurring factors of this world: the lust of the flesh, lust of the eyes and the pride of life are not labeled as sin. 1 John 2:15-17 tells us that it is the love of them and the world that is a sin. The love being spoken of here is a matter of preference not a feeling. So, to choose or prefer to yield your will to such as Adam and Eve did instead of yielding it to the divine nature as Christ did, is what is a sin. We must not allow these factors to entice us to prefer them when they are in opposition to God's divine nature. 1 John 2:17 makes the reason clear, they will pass one day but God's will is eternal. We also will live eternally if we abide by his will. Because man yielded their will to human nature and proved that their love for the world eclipsed their love for God, they fell. With that being said, we have the reason that Christ had to learn obedience. The first man Adam failed to trust God and his lack of obedience proved where his love was. Now the second man Jesus Christ, had to prove his love through obedience by trusting God. Due to the susceptibility of the will to the influence of human nature, tribulation is a necessity. So, while it says that he learned obedience by suffering, since it is a type of it, we can also say that it was by tribulation.

What he Suffered

Since he was tempted in all points as we are let's go over his experiences that lead to his obedience.

Being Misunderstood

Often parents fail to acknowledge the truth of what they see before them. It is for this reason that they will assume that their tween or teen is just like all the others at their age. This results in limitations and a certain manner of overprotection at times. The point is as parents when we realize a deeper level of maturity being expressed at an earlier age that we tend to subconsciously fear and reject it at times. I'm persuaded that it is a result of the fact that they will leave the nest one day and depend on us less. The fear is more so one that we will no longer be needed. As a result, we may overlook this difference by treating our children in a manner that they find demeaning and their maturity is not recognized in our verbal interactions. Therefore, the child is hurt and feels misunderstood. In Luke 2:41-52 we have the account of Jesus being left behind when he was 12. While Mary and Joseph were told by the angel that her child was not like every other child, she still treated him no differently. In Luke 2:40 we see that they witnessed the evidence of this difference daily, in his growth in grace, wisdom and spirituality. In spite of this, upon their journey home they casually assumed that he was among the other children. They thought that surely, he was doing what the other 12-year-old boys his age would be doing and considered nothing of it. Because of this error it took a whole day for them to realize that he was missing and three more to find him. Once he was located, they still failed to accept what they had witnessed for 12 years. The result in Luke 2:48 was Jesus being chastised for his supposed folly that was expected of a child his age. Listen to the hurt in his voice in Luke 2:49, evidence of his hurt at their lack of being unable to accept his level of maturity that they were well aware of. Either way whether we are an adult, or a child Jesus knows what it is like to be misunderstood.

Rejection

Throughout his earthly ministry Jesus experienced a lot of rejection. This was in spite of the fact that the works that he did was literal proof of his authenticity.

Have you ever proved your worth over and over only to be rejected?

If so, Christ understands. We see this in these passages in Luke 4:17-24. In John 6:48-66 when Jesus explained that he was the bread of life. His explanation was not received and much of the multitude that followed him refused to follow him any longer. Prior to this they were eager to accept him but sought proof so that they might believe as we see in John 6:28-34. In John 6:35-40 he gave them their proof, but the Jews would not receive it and mocked him as it shows in John 6:41,42. Realize that just a day before this that Jesus had fed the 5,000 plus.

Perhaps the greatest rejection is in the guise of a person not being thankful. You pour out your heart and soul into some beneficial service only for it to be taken for granted. After Jesus healed the demoniac in Mark 5:16,17, who had troubled the locals, considering that they tried binding him and calming him unsuccessfully, they prayed for Jesus to depart. After all the miracles of healing the sick, raising the dead and feeding the hungry when the people held his fate in their hands, they chose to crucify him and set a murderer free. This was the gratitude expressed to the incarnate of love and one of the reasons in which he learned obedience. It was a matter of whether our forerunner would yield to human nature and become bitter and resentful or if he would yield to the divine nature and forgive. We know from reading Luke

23:34 that he yielded to the divine nature, regardless of any justification presented by human nature to hold the offense against them.

Sorrow

At some point we all are overtaken with grief and overwhelmed with sorrow. As we have discussed it is not a sin for a Christian to undergo such emotions. We also discussed the points at which these lower levels of pride become sin. They become sin when we are wholly given over to unbelief. It is a natural occurrence of our human nature for us to deal with such emotions. This is true for both sinner and saint alike and it is also inevitable. With that said, neither could Jesus circumvent this experience. In Isaiah 53:3-5 it tells us 3 He is despised and rejected of men a man of sorrows, and acquainted with grief: and we hid as it were our faces from him; he was despised, and we esteemed him not. 4 Surely, he hath borne our griefs, and carried our sorrows: yet we did esteem him stricken, smitten of God, and afflicted.

In the Garden of Gethsemane, we see the greatest display of this sorrow. Matthew 26:37,38 tells us that he was exceedingly sorrowful, even to the point of death. During this time with strong crying and tears he prayed unto God as it reads in Hebrews 5:7. This place was a location for stomping grapes underfoot until the juice was pressed out. In Luke 22:44 it tells us that Christ was under such duress that the weight upon his soul pressed blood from his pores. It was not his imminent Crucifixion that brought about this sorrow, Hebrews 12:2 tells us that this was part of the joy set before him. Within this same verse it also speaks of the shame that he despised. The shame was the inevitable rejection of the Father that he would experience. This rejection would take place as he exchanged his righteousness for our sin and took our sin upon himself as it reads in 2 Corinthians 5:21. Everything he did was to please the Father, so to be rejected by the Father or even shame him would bring him the greatest sorrow. Yet his humanity would not be complete without the experience of feeling the rejection of God due to sin as is found in Isaiah 59:1,2. So it would be this cup that he so desired not to drink of. This was the Achilles heel human nature would seize in order to subjugate his soul but through prayer he would humble himself and reign in his human nature under the authority of the divine nature.

Pain

No one takes pleasure in undergoing excruciating pain or most pain in general. As Christians some of our greatest misunderstandings with God's love is his allowance for us to endure pain. We wonder how he could watch as we are hurting and why at times he delays in his intervention, if at all. Jesus himself as God and man understands those same thoughts. At the cruel hands of the Roman soldiers, it is a safe bet that the full wrath of Satan was unleashed. He was not just scourged, an experience so brutal that many did not survive but Psalms 22:17 tells us that his flesh was torn to the degree that his bones were exposed. Isaiah 52:14 goes on to explain that Christ was disfigured more than any man. Aside from spitting on him and hitting him as we see in Mark 14:65, Isaiah 50:6 says that they plucked his beard and in Matthew 27:27-30 says that they beat a crown of thorns into his head. Not only did God stand by and watch but he was pleased by what he saw. God was especially pleased with the culmination of this, the nailing of Christ's broken body to the cross.

How cruel and unloving for God to do so, right?

It is quite the opposite as we read in Isaiah 53:10,11, 10 Yet it pleased the Lord to bruise him; he hath put him to grief: when thou shalt make his soul an offering for sin, he shall see his seed, he shall prolong his days, and the pleasure of the Lord shall prosper in his hand. 11 He shall see of the travail of his soul and shall be satisfied: by his knowledge shall my righteous servant justify many; for he shall bear their iniquities. So, we realize that God was pleased with what the pain that Christ endured would yield, not his experiencing of it. We must also understand, that the painful moments that try our faith are precious unto God as it says in 1 Peter 1:7. Like with Christ he knows what and how long is enough for his purpose to be fulfilled.

We realize that by Christ rejecting the lure of his human nature to captivate his will and instead yielding to the divine nature by trusting in

God, that this resulted in obedience. His obedience is what proved his love for God. Without undergoing tribulation that is common to man, not only could he not fully understand our humanity, but neither could he prove his love for God. Christ did not only learn obedience by tribulation, but he also showed us an example of how to allow tribulation to help us do the same.

CHAPTER 12

En Garde

At the end of chapter 3 I expressed that the indwelling of the Holy Ghost was never meant by God to be the culmination of our salvation experience. Upon conversion, the main purpose of the indwelling of the Holy Ghost is to regenerate the soul that is dead in trespasses and sin. It is from there that the soul is baptized into the Body of Christ and through the indwelling of the Holy Ghost Jesus and the Father make their abode within us. It is by the indwelling of the Holy Ghost that the Fruits of the Spirit also abide in us. As we exercise these fruits, we have no shame before God as Romans 5:5 tells us due to love. Romans 13:8 - 10 explains the reason why we will have no shame. It is because love fulfills the law and works no ill toward its neighbor. This is why the first greatest commandment is to love God with all of our heart, soul and mind and the second is to love your neighbor as yourself as is found in Matthew 22:37-40. In this state alone the salvation experience is incomplete and the same goes for water baptism. In this state you have been cleansed of sin and have answered unto a good conscience and partaken of the death burial and resurrection of Jesus Christ but there is a missing step. It is that missing step which Christ himself was a partaker of and desires for all who come unto him also to partake, thus making the salvation experience complete.

We will use fencing as an analogy to convey this point:

1. In a very generalized perspective fencing is a series of movements in which two individuals engage each other in combat conducting a series of advance and retreat movements.

2. The initial stance is en garde. This is the defensive stance both parties assume.

3. Next both parties advance initiating a series of thrusts, which are well thought out jabbing pokes performed with precision. These thrusts are meant to probe for openings in the opponent's defense so that a point can be scored.

4. In response to an attack the other party retreats backward and fends with a parry that blocks the attack. Then they try to counter and advance forward sending the opponent into retreat as they seek to gain the advantage.

This series of advances and retreats will continue until the final blow has been delivered, thus the victor is decided. The indwelling of the Holy Ghost received at salvation places the newly converted believer in en garde. When the soul was dead it was powerless to defend against human nature and its master, the devil. The newly regenerated soul is free and also is equipped with armor as we read in Ephesians 6:10-18 and weapons as seen in 2 Corinthians 10:3-6. Those weapons and armor places that converted soul in the en garde stance as you see in these passages Matthew 26:41; Philippians 2:12, Ephesians 5:15-17. Now the soul has the power and ability to be wary of the advances of human nature and the power to fight back. Because the body remains unconverted, human nature will advance with probing thrusts, searching for an opening to pierce us until we have been slain once more. These openings in which we are pierced are infirmities, areas we need growth in spiritual fruits and things not wholly yielded to God and such. We parry through prayer, bible reading, meditating on the bible, singing praises, church attendance and the like. We advance and counter with things such as faith, prayer, bible reading, fellowship, encouraging ourselves in the Lord and going to church.

However, the indwelling of the Holy Ghost does not give us the ability to deal that decisive blow. As a result, we succeed at gaining points and driving the enemy back, but the match is never decided, so the wearisome dance continues. After a while, the believer may feel like they are going through an endless loop of gaining ground but never achieving lasting victory. You may have felt like there has to be more to serving God than this. In time you will find your will weakened and assailed by human natures influence. Then once more your soul will die as it is drawn back into bondage and your freedom of will is lost.

Coup de Grace

Realize that for the believer the baptism of the Holy Ghost is our coup de grace.

This word means:

- A stroke of mercy.
- Death blow.
- Final decisive stroke.

The Holy Ghost baptism is the culmination of our salvation experience and without it we are incomplete. It is our ultimate strategy from God against those forces of spiritual wickedness we read of in Ephesians 6:12, that stir our human nature against our will. For a believer it is a stroke of mercy as it enables us with true power to overcome our human nature. The Holy Ghost baptism is the part of the salvation experience by which we become partakers of the power of Jesus Christ. It was this same power that was the corner stone of the ministry of Christ and by which he evoked every miracle. We activate this power by stirring up this gift as a poker does to the embers of an old fire place, read 2 Timothy 1:6,7. It is the Holy Ghost baptism experience that is received by laying on of hands. The receipt of that gift by laying on of hands is the same gift spoken of in the ordeal with Peter rebuking the sorcerer in Acts 8:14-24 that Paul was speaking of, when he addressed Timothy. Peter rebuked the sorcerer because he desired to purchase the ability to distribute the Holy Ghost baptism by laying on of hands for monetary gain. We stir up this gift by building ourselves up on our most holy faith by praying in the Holy Ghost as seen in Jude 20. Jude 21 tells us that by praying in the Holy Ghost we keep ourselves in the love of God. When we pray in the Holy Ghost, we edify ourselves. 1 Corinthians 14:2,4 tells us that we are edified when we allow the Spirit to pray through us with unknown tongues. For Satan, spiritual forces, wickedness in high places and our human nature, the Holy Ghost baptism is a deathblow and final decisive moment. It gives us the victory when the enemy comes in like a flood, read Isaiah 59:19. As we stir up this gift and apply God's word, this enables the Spirit to act on our behalf. We must seek the baptism of the Holy Ghost as a believer because it is a separate portion of our salvation experience, read Luke 11:13. We have learned that aside from asking that this gift is received by the laying on of hands. John the Baptist made the proclamation that Jesus would baptize with the Holy Ghost and with fire, not water read Luke 3:16,17. Jesus told the disciples that once he rose again and ascended that he would ask the Father to send another Comforter read John 14:16 and that Comforter was the Holy Ghost as we see in John 14:26. Then Jesus proclaimed in Acts 1:4,5, though John baptized with water that they would be baptized with the Holy Ghost and once they received it, that they would receive power, read Acts 1:8. The initial sign that the power was received was the recipient speaking in unknown tongues as is seen in the following scriptures Acts 2:1-4, Acts 10:44-48;Acts 19:1-6.

When Jesus spoke of the Comforter to come, whom the Father would send and they would be baptized of and receive power from, he was not speaking of the indwelling of the Holy Ghost that is received at salvation. Jesus told them that they knew the Spirit of truth because he dwelled with them and would be in them read John 14:17. The disciples already had the indwelling of the Spirit, which regenerated their soul and they were already baptized with water. Even so Jesus commanded them to tarry at Jerusalem until they received power, the Holy Ghost baptism. This would thereby complete their salvation experience.

The Holy Ghost baptism equips us with the tools to properly maintain our salvation experience. One of those tools is praying in the Holy

Ghost in which the Spirit prays through us with unknown tongues and builds us up on our most holy faith or prays in our stead with groaning, read Romans 8:26. It is by daily praying in tongues that we stir up this gift, keeping the flames fanned so that the chaff in our hearts may be consumed as we read in Matthew 3:11,12. Also with those infirmities that plague us it is through praying in the Holy Ghost that God administers help to aide us, read Romans 8:26,27, along with what we discussed at the end of chapter 8.

Our Example

Jesus did not take on a body just for empathy but to show us how to overcome bondage to our human nature. The Holy Ghost baptism is the power that gave the man Jesus Christ the ability to learn obedience by the things that he suffered. We have already discussed that Jesus was full God and full man. However, he was baptized with the Holy Ghost to conquer the man, his human nature, that was a result of the soul that resided in his earthly body. After his water baptism he was baptized with the Holy Ghost who descended upon him in a physical form like it did upon those in the upper room, read Matthew 3:16. The experience with him was gentle because unlike the disciples there was no chaff to burn from Christ because he had no sin. After receiving this power, he began his ministry just as he admonished the disciples after his resurrection to wait until they received the same before the church would advance with the gospel. Every miracle he did was accomplished by this power. Every tribulation he endured was faced with this power. Not only did the Spirit lead Christ into the wilderness as we read in Matthew 4:1 but it taught him and empowered him to overcome the temptations of Satan, read 1 John 2:27. When grieved by the unbelief of the people Jesus groaned in the Spirit as we see in John 11:33,38. When he healed Jairus' daughter he spoke in an unknown tongue, read Mark 5:40-43. So as Christ was tempted in all points as we are, through Holy Ghost power he showed us how to overcome temptation and made it available to everyone, read Acts 2:38,39.

ABOUT THE AUTHOR

J.A. Cox is a Christian, disabled veteran, husband and father. His greatest passion is his belief in Jesus Christ who drives him to live a life that is pleasing unto him and does his best to allow him to be seen in the things that he does. While he has gone through many things and failed in many ways along the way, the power of God's love has become more real to him. He has come to learn that the love of God is like a tsunami that hits you like a feather. It means the magnitude of his love is overwhelming in its expanse but when it engulfs you as it washes away the filth it does not destroy you in the process but it is a gentle, warm and peaceful experience.

www.ingramcontent.com/pod-product-compliance
Lightning Source LLC
Chambersburg PA
CBHW060341130626
46553CB00003B/1076